CliffsNotes™

Frankenstein

By Jeff Coghill

IN THIS BOOK

- Learn about the Life and Background of the Author
- Preview an Introduction to the Novel
- Explore themes, style and language, and literary devices in the Critical Commentaries
- Delve into in-depth Character Analyses
- Gain an understanding of the novel with Critical Essays
- Reinforce what you learn with CliffsNotes Review
- Find additional information to further your study in the CliffsNotes Resource Center and online at www.cliffsnotes.com

WILEY

Wiley Publishing, Inc.

About the Author

Currently a librarian and instructor of English at McNeese State University in Lake Charles, LA, Jeff Coghill grew up an Army brat and graduated in 1980 from Heidelberg American High School in Heidelberg, Germany. He went on to earn his B.A. in English from Methodist College in 1983, his M.A. in English from Western Carolina University, and his M.L.I.S. in library studies from the University of Alabama in 1997. He now resides in Lake Charles, LA with his wife, Michele; his teenage daughter, Caroline; and his West Highland White Terrier, "Alfie" a.k.a. Alfred, Lord Tennyson.

Publisher's Acknowledgments
Editorial

Senior Project Editor: Colleen Williams Esterline
Acquisitions Editor: Greg Tubach
Copy Editor: Colleen Williams Esterline
Glossary Editors: The editors and staff of Webster's New World Dictionaries

Composition

Indexer: York Production Services, Inc.
Proofreader: York Production Services, Inc.
Wiley Indianapolis Composition Services

CliffsNotes™ *Frankenstein*

Published by:
Wiley Publishing, Inc.
111 River Street
Hoboken, NJ 07030
www.wiley.com

Copyright © 2001 Wiley Publishing, Inc., Hoboken, NJ
ISBN: 978-0-7645-8593-7
Printed in the United States of America
15 14 13 12
1O/TR/RQ/QT/IN
Published by Wiley Publishing, Inc., Hoboken, NJ
Published simultaneously in Canada

Library of Congress Cataloging-in-Publication Data
Coghill, Jeff.
  CliffsNotes Shelley's Frankenstein / Jeff Coghill.
    p. cm.
  Includes index.
  ISBN 978-0-7645-8593-7 (alk. paper)
  1. Shelley, Mary Wollstonecraft, 1797-1851. Frankenstein--Examinations--Study guides. 3. Horror tales, English--Examinations--Study guides. 4. Scientists in literature. 5. Monsters in literature.
I. Title: Frankenstein. II. Title
PR5397.F73 C64 2000
823.7--dc21   00–037036
                                                        CIP

Table of Contents

LIfe and Background of the Author 1
Personal Background 2
Career Highlights 4

Introduction to the Novel 5
Introduction to the Novel 6
Brief Synopsis 8
List of Characters 10
Character Map 12

Critical Commentaries 13
Preface to the 1817 Edition 14
Introduction to the 1831 Edition 15
Letter 1: To Mrs. Saville, England 16
  Summary 16
  Commentary 16
Letter 2: To Mrs. Saville, England 18
  Summary 18
  Commentary 18
Letter 3: To Mrs. Saville, England 19
  Summary 19
  Commentary 19
Letter 4: To Mrs. Saville, England 20
  Summary 20
  Commentary 20
  Glossary 22
Chapter 1 23
  Summary 23
  Commentary 23
  Glossary 24
Chapter 2 25
  Summary 25
  Commentary 25
  Glossary 27
Chapter 3 28
  Summary 28
  Commentary 28
Chapter 4 30
  Summary 30
  Commentary 30
  Glossary 32
Chapter 5 33
  Summary 33
  Commentary 33

Chapter 6 35
    Summary 35
    Commentary 35
Chapter 7 37
    Summary 37
    Commentary 37
Chapter 8 39
    Summary 39
    Commentary 39
    Glossary 40
Chapter 9 41
    Summary 41
    Commentary 41
    Glossary 42
Chapter 10 43
    Summary 43
    Commentary 43
    Glossary 44
Chapter 11 45
    Summary 45
    Commentary 45
    Glossary 46
Chapter 12 47
    Summary 47
    Commentary 47
Chapter 13 48
    Summary 48
    Commentary 48
Chapter 14 50
    Summary 50
    Commentary 50
Chapter 15 51
    Summary 51
    Commentary 51
    Glossary 52
Chapter 16 53
    Summary 53
    Commentary 53
Chapter 17 54
    Summary 54
    Commentary 54
Chapter 18 55
    Summary 55
    Commentary 55

Chapter 19 56
    Summary 56
    Commentary 56
Chapter 20 57
    Summary 57
    Commentary 57
Chapter 21 59
    Summary 59
    Commentary 59
Chapter 22 60
    Summary 60
    Commentary 60
Chapter 23 61
    Summary 61
    Commentary 61
    Glossary 62
Chapter 24 63
    Summary 63
    Commentary 63
Final Letters 65
    Summary 65
    Commentary 66

Character Analyses . . . . **.67**
    Victor Frankenstein 68
    The monster 68
    Elizabeth Lavenza 69
    Justine Moritz 69

Critical Essays . . . . **.70**
    Themes 71
    The Romantic Movement 72
    The Gothic Novel 73
    Plot 75

CliffsNotes Review . . . . **.76**

CliffsNotes Resource Center . . . . **.80**

Index . . . . **.83**

How to Use This Book

This CliffsNotes study guide on Mary Shelley's *Frankenstein* supplements the original literary work, giving you background information about the author, an introduction to the work, a graphical character map, critical commentaries, expanded glossaries, and a comprehensive index, all for you to use as an educational tool that will allow you to better understand *Frankenstein*. This study guide was written with the assumption that you have read *Frankenstein*. Reading a literary work doesn't mean that you immediately grasp the major themes and devices used by the author; this study guide will help supplement your reading to be sure you get all you can from Mary Shelley's *Frankenstein*. CliffsNotes Review tests your comprehension of the original text and reinforces learning with questions and answers, practice projects, and more. For further information on Mary Shelley and *Frankenstein*, check out the CliffsNotes Resource Center.

CliffsNotes provides the following icons to highlight essential elements of particular interest:

Reveals the underlying themes in the work.

Helps you to more easily relate to or discover the depth of a character.

Uncovers elements such as setting, atmosphere, mystery, passion, violence, irony, symbolism, tragedy, foreshadowing, and satire.

Enables you to appreciate the nuances of words and phrases.

Don't Miss Our Web Site

Discover classic literature as well as modern-day treasures by visiting the Cliffs-Notes Web site at www.cliffsnotes.com. You can obtain a quick download of a CliffsNotes title, purchase a title in print form, browse our catalog, or view online samples.

LIFE AND BACKGROUND OF THE AUTHOR

The following abbreviated biography of Mary Shelley is provided so that you might become more familiar with her life and the historical times that possibly influenced her writing. Read this Life and Background of the Author section and recall it when reading Shelley's *Frankenstein*, thinking of any thematic relationship between Shelley's novel and her life.

Personal Background 2

Career Highlights 4

Personal Background

Mary Wollstonecraft (Godwin) Shelley was born on August 30, 1797 in London, England to philosopher William Godwin and feminist Mary Wollstonecraft; both her parents were noted writers in the 1800s. Her father's most famous book was *Political Justice* (1793), which is a critical look at society and the ethical treatment of the masses. Godwin's other popular book *Caleb Williams* (1794) examines class distinctions and the misuse of power by the ruling aristocracy. Mary Wollstonecraft, her mother, was a leading feminist writer who espoused her views in her famous work *A Vindication of the Rights of Women* (1792). They married in 1797 to protect the rights of the forthcoming child. When their daughter Mary was born, William and Mary had only been married for five months. Four weeks after giving birth, Mary Wollstonecraft died of complications. Thus, Mary Shelley never knew her mother. Her father remarried a woman by the name of Mrs. Clairmont when the young Mary was four years old.

Mary's learned father, who had frequent guests in their home all through her formative years, guaranteed her education. A voracious reader, Mary borrowed books from her father's extensive library. She enjoyed writing at a young age, and her passion was to write stories intended for a very limited audience. The influence of her famous father's home cannot be understated with a constant stream of writers, including Samuel Taylor Coleridge. It was at home that Mary developed into a person of letters, following in the family tradition of writers and thinkers.

Between June 1812 and March 1814, Mary lived with relatives in Scotland. It was upon her return visits to London when she met Percy Bysshe Shelley, who idolized her father, and their relationship began. Mary and Percy left England for France in June 1814 to begin a life together. Shelley was still married to his first wife, Harriet Westbrook. Within four years of being married, Percy met Mary, and a new marriage was proposed as soon as the first marriage was dissolved. In late 1814, Mary and Percy returned to England and lived in hiding to avoid his first wife and previous back debts. It was at this time that Percy petitioned Mary's father William for relief of his debt.

In February 1815, Mary gave birth to a daughter, who was born prematurely and who subsequently died in March of the same year. The couple settled in Bishopgate, England and a second child, William, was born.

In the summer of 1816, a tour of continental Europe was proposed. At a stop in Switzerland, the couple and Mary's stepsister, Claire, rented a house near another British writer, Lord Byron. The summer proved wet and unseasonable; Byron suggested the group take to writing ghost stories to pass the time. It was during this summer that the form for *Frankenstein* was to take shape. The story was first only a few pages, but with the encouragement of Percy, the tale took on a greater length. Mary's story, the best of the group, was so frightening to Byron that he ran "shrieking in horror" from the room. Frankenstein was published in 1818.

In November 1816, Fanny, Mary's half-sister, committed suicide. A few weeks later, in December 1816, Shelley's first wife Harriet also killed herself. Within two weeks, Percy and Mary were married in St. Mildred's Church in London on December 30, 1816. Early the next year, the couple moved to Marlow, England and a third child, Clara Everina, was born. In 1818, the Shelley's left England for Italy to escape mounting debt and to improve Percy's health. It was during this time that both small children died; Clara died in September 1818, and William died the following June, in 1819. Mary was miserable and disconsolate at 21 and 22 years of age. She did recover somewhat later in November 1819 when her son Percy was born in Florence, Italy. He would become the only Shelley child to survive to adulthood. Mary did not remain idle as a writer during this time, as she began a new novel, *Valperga*.

On July 8, 1822, Mary's life was forever altered when her husband was drowned at sea in a boating accident off the coast of Livorno (sometimes called Leghorn), Italy. By now, her life was seemingly connected to tragedy, with the deaths of three children, her mother, and her husband, and the suicides of Percy's former wife and Mary's half-sister.

She spent the rest of her life writing original works and tending to the works of her late husband. She became the keeper of Percy Bysshe Shelley's fame and was editor of his posthumous works. This was done to raise the necessary funds to support herself and her son. In 1824, *Posthumous Poems* was published, which was edited by Mary. She had begun negotiations with her father-in-law, Sir Timothy Shelley, who did not want his son's works published or his family's name published in the press again during his lifetime. *The Last Man* (1826) is Shelley's best-known work after *Frankenstein* because it tackles the subject of mass catastrophe in society.

In 1841, her son graduated from Trinity College, and he asked his mother to accompany him on a tour of Italy and Europe. During her trip, she compiled notes about her travels. Her son married in 1848, and Mary lived with him and his wife until she died. On February 1, 1851 Mary died in London and was buried in Bournemouth, England.

Career Highlights

The first and most memorable work of Mary Shelley is her creation of *Frankenstein*, which she wrote during the summer of 1816 and published in 1818.

The sophomore novel of Shelley was *Valperga*. Mary returned to England in August 1823 to "find myself famous" with the reception of *Valperga* and a stage adaptation of *Frankenstein*. *The Last Man* (1826) is Shelley's best-known work after *Frankenstein* because it tackles the subject of mass catastrophe in society.

From 1829 to 1839, Mary began writing articles and stories for the *Westminster Review*, *The Keepsake*, and other publications. She worked again on her own novels and wrote notes to accompany her husband's works. During this period *The Life and Adventures of Castruccio, Prince of Lucca* (1823), *The Fortunes of Perkin Warbeck* (1830), *Lodore* (1835), and *Falkner* (1837) were all published. However, none would achieve the success and recognition that her earliest and best novel would achieve. By 1844, she had amassed enough notes from her travels with her son to publish them in two volumes called *Rambles in Germany and Italy* (1844).

INTRODUCTION TO THE NOVEL

The following Introduction section is provided solely as an educational tool and is not meant to replace the experience of your reading the novel. Read the Introduction and A Brief Synopsis to enhance your understanding of the novel and to prepare yourself for the critical thinking that should take place whenever you read any work of fiction or non-fiction. Keep the List of Characters and Character Map at hand so that as you read the original literary work, if you encounter a character about whom you're uncertain, you can refer to the List of Characters and Character Map to refresh your memory.

Introduction to the Novel 6

Brief Synopsis 8

List of Characters 10

Character Map .12

Introduction to the Novel

Frankenstein is a unique novel in the canon of English literature. The novel seeks to find the answers to questions that no doubt perplexed Mary Shelley and the readers of her time.

Shelley presents a unique character in Victor Frankenstein and his creation, the monster. It is as though there are two distinct halves to one character. Each half competes for attention from the other and for the chance to be the ruler of the other half. In the end, this competition reduces both men to ruins.

Shelley also is keenly aware of the concern that technology was advancing at a rate that dizzied the mind of early eighteenth century readers. Perhaps this novel is addressing that issue of advances created by men, but which fly in the face of "natural" elements and divine plans.

Mary Shelley crafts her exquisite novel in a way to direct attention to the treatment of the poor and uneducated as a major theme throughout the book. She would have learned these precepts from her father William Godwin, a noted writer and philosopher. (Refer to the "Life and Background of the Author" section.) But the beginnings of the historical background go back much further than Shelley's own time.

To understand Shelley's time period, one must delve into the period that preceded Shelley's. Mary was born in 1797, after the American and French Revolutions. Europe was a tense place for fear of potential political revolutions during much of the period from 1770–1800. The English upper class feared that the French Revolution might spill over to their own country. Many felt that change was necessary to ensure equality among the masses. The wars that Napoleon waged, begun in 1805, essentially quashed any real hope of building a better Europe. However, the seeds of discord were sown for the dissolution of social and class barriers in England and mainland Europe. The cries of "liberty, fraternity, and equality," were left on the impressionable minds of men everywhere. It was thought that man could achieve greater personal liberty, without the threat of overbearing governments. Men also reasoned that brotherhood in a common cause—whether it be social, class, or academic—would lead to a better country and a better government.

England benefited from being linked to Europe, but the English Channel served to slow the pace of the revolution that swept the European continent. English political and social institutions were keenly aware of the wave of feelings that revolution had created in France and the United States. Since English rule was now less dependent on the monarchy than before, the power structure of the United Kingdom was more widely distributed than her European counterparts. The balance that England achieved made for an uneasy peace at home. England was at war with France from 1793 to 1815. The English government made deals with other monarchs in Prussia, Russia, and Austria to keep England from entering into any alliance that might compromise English control of the high seas. The result was criticism of English foreign policy at home by such liberal thinkers such as Lord Byron and Percy Shelley. Both of these men had seen the results of England's turning the other cheek from the repression that they saw in Austria and Italy. Byron and Shelley felt that the Tory party in England had not done enough to ensure the freedom of the people at large and had essentially "gotten in bed" with the more conservative Austrians and Italians.

The Industrial Revolution also gave rise to a new social class in European society, the middle class. As more businesses moved from home- or cottage-based operations, factories became the next place where conflict would be waged between the working poor and their employers. New towns sprang up with a new set of problems for local governments. Few checks and balances existed for factory owners or governments. As a result, town life was forbidding and dangerous. The countryside yielded little relief from city life, as small farmers had to make a living on small plots of land, in contrast to large landowners. Usually, the old gentries had ruled the land for many years previous, and they controlled the larger portions of land, thus regulating its use. The poor enjoyed a better standard of living than previously, but the concerns of the poor and the gap between the rich and poor became more pronounced during this period.

The English government repressed the people at home, fearing a latent revolution and fearing the liberals in the government who supported social and economic reforms. Mary Shelley writes about the ideal society where people aided each other and the less fortunate. Liberal-minded men would ensure that the conditions of those who labored on the farm or in the factory would be tolerable and fair. The Shelley's, both Mary and Percy, adopted these ideas. The proper treatment of the Frankenstein's housekeeper, Justine Moritz, is indicative of Mary's own views of how the laboring class should be treated. Also, the whole De Lacey story line details the French government's imprisonment and banishment, for unclear reasons, of a family who aided a Turkish merchant in their home country. As a result of their assistance, the family has all of their possessions confiscated, and the male members of the family are sent to prison. Shelley suggests that governments are too powerful and that charges of treason are too easily leveled, without the benefit of a proper trial and circumstantial evidence. The savior is Safie, who uses her own wealth to rescue the De Lacey's from certain poverty.

Brief Synopsis

The novel begins with explorer Robert Walton looking for a new passage from Russia to the Pacific Ocean via the Arctic Ocean. After weeks as sea, the crew of Walton's ship finds an emaciated man, Victor Frankenstein, floating on an ice flow near death. In Walton's series of letters to his sister in England, he retells Victor's tragic story.

Growing up in Geneva, Switzerland, Victor is a precocious child, quick to learn all new subjects. He is raised with Elizabeth, an orphan adopted by his family. Victor delights in the sciences and vows to some-day study science. Victor prepares to leave for his studies at the University of Ingolstadt, when his mother and Elizabeth become ill with scarlet fever. Caroline dies from the disease, and Elizabeth is nursed back to health.

At the university, Victor meets his professors M. Krempe and M. Waldman. For two years, Victor becomes very involved with his stud-ies, even impressing his teachers and fellow students. He devises a plan to re-create and reanimate a dead body. He uses a combination of chem-istry, alchemy, and electricity to make his ambition a reality.

After bringing the creature to life, Victor feels guilty that he has brought a new life into the world with no provisions for taking care of the "monster." He runs away in fear and disgust from his creation and his conscience. The monster wanders the countryside while Victor seeks solace in a tavern near the university. Henry Clerval appears to save Vic-tor and restore him to health.

Alphonse writes to Victor telling him to come home immediately since an unknown assailant murdered his youngest brother, William, by strangulation. Justine Moritz, their housekeeper, is falsely accused of the murder of William, and she goes to the gallows willingly. Victor knows who the killer is but cannot tell his family or the police. He jour-neys out of Geneva to refresh his tortured soul and visits Mount Mon-tanvert when he sees the monster coming to confront his maker with a proposition—"make me a mate of my own." Victor refuses, and the monster asks that his part of the story be heard. The pair retreats to a small hut on the mountain where the monster tells his story.

The monster has taught himself to read and understand language so that he can follow the lives of his "adopted" family, the De Laceys. While the monster wanders the woods, he comes upon a jacket with a notebook and letters that were lost by Victor. From the notes, the monster learns of his creation. He has endured rejection by mankind, but he has not retaliated upon mankind in general for his misfortune. Instead, he has decided to take revenge on his creator's family to avenge the injury and sorrow he endures from others.

Victor refuses to make a second monster, but is convinced when the monster assures Victor that he will leave Europe and move to South America. Victor agrees to begin work on a second creation and makes plans to go to England and Scotland, with Henry Clerval, to begin his secret work. Before he leaves Geneva, Victor agrees to marry Elizabeth immediately upon his return from the British Isles. Victor takes up residence in the Orkney Islands, off the coast of Scotland. Victor destroys his project and goes out to sea to dispose of the remains. The monster vows revenge on Victor for not upholding his end of their bargain.

While at sea, Victor's boat is blown off course by a sudden storm, and he ends up in Ireland. Henry Clerval's body has washed up on the shores of Ireland, and Victor is set to stand trail for murder. Fortunately, Mr. Kirwin, a local magistrate, intercedes on Victor's behalf and pleads his case before a court, which then finds Victor innocent of the crime. Victor is miserable knowing he has caused the deaths of so many, but recovers enough to finalize the plans for his marriage to Elizabeth.

With a wedding date set, Victor torments himself with the thought of the monster's threat to be with him on his wedding night. The wedding goes off as planned. While Victor makes sure he covers all possible entrances that the monster could use to get into the wedding chamber, the monster steals into Elizabeth's room and strangles her.

Victor now wants revenge and chases the monster through Europe and Russia. Victor nearly catches the monster near the Arctic Circle when Robert Walton discovers him. Victor, now near death, is taken aboard Walton's ship to recover from exhaustion and exposure.

The monster appears out of the mists and ice to visit his foe one last time. The monster enters the cabin of the ship and tells Walton his side of the story. Victor dies, and the monster tells Walton that he will burn his own funeral pyre. The monster then disappears in the waves and darkness, never to be seen again.

List of Characters

Victor Frankenstein Creator of the monster. Victor becomes obsessed with the idea of creating the human form and acts upon it. Immediately after creating the monster, he falls into a depression and fear. He leaves the school and returns home to his family, only to find tragedy there. Not fully aware of the consequences of his creating a new human, he spends his entire life trying to destroy the same creation.

The monster The creature created by Victor Frankenstein while at the University of Ingolstadt. "Formed into a hideous and gigantic creature," the monster faces rejection and fear from his creator and society. The monster's rejection from society pushes him to commit murder against his creator's family.

Henry Clerval Victor's best friend who helps Victor in his time of need. The monster kills Henry after Victor breaks his promise of creating a female companion for the monster. He studies language at the University of Ingolstadt and is totally unaware of Victor's creation.

Elizabeth Lavenza The orphan child taken in by the Frankenstein family and lovingly raised with Victor. Elizabeth later becomes Victor's wife and is killed by the monster on their honeymoon. She is a champion for the poor and underpriviledged.

Alphonse Frankenstein Victor's father. He suffers from illness probably brought on from his advanced age and depression from the events that have happened.

Caroline Beaufort Frankenstein Victor's mother. Caroline dies of scarlet fever when Victor is 17. Caroline was very involved in charity work—much like Mary Shelley and her mother Mary Wollstonecraft—especially for families in poverty.

William Frankenstein Victor's youngest brother who is killed by the monster. Symbolically, William's murder is the turning point of the novel, when turmoil engulfs the Frankenstein family and all innocence is lost in the family. Also, William's death signals for the reader the end of Victor's belief that his actions can have no consequences.

Justine Moritz The housekeeper for the Frankenstein family. Accused of William's murder, Justine is the stolid martyr who goes to her death with grace and dignity. If William's death symbolizes the loss of innocence, Justine's death marks the end of all that is noble and righteous.

The De Lacey family M. De Lacey, Felix, Agatha, and Safie. The monster's adopted family. Exiled from France for treason against their government.

Robert Walton Arctic explorer on his way to find a Northwest Passage through the Arctic Ocean from Russia to the Pacific Ocean. Robert finds Victor Frankenstein near death, listens to his tale, and records it in letters to his sister Margaret Saville.

Margaret Saville Robert's sister. Robert writes to her detailing the events that transpire on the voyage and Victor's story.

Character Map

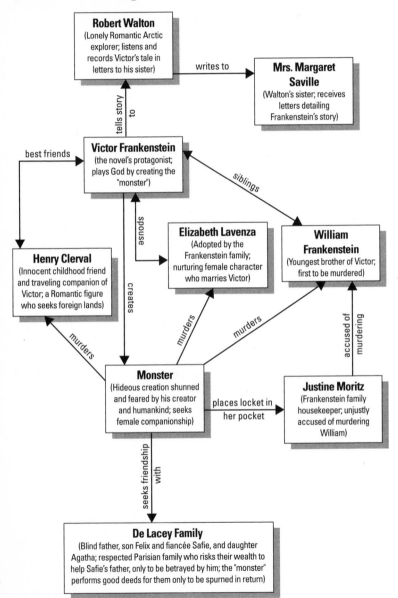

Robert Walton
(Lonely Romantic Arctic explorer; listens and records Victor's tale in letters to his sister)

writes to

Mrs. Margaret Saville
(Walton's sister; receives letters detailing Frankenstein's story)

tells story to

Victor Frankenstein
(the novel's protagonist; plays God by creating the "monster")

best friends

siblings

spouse

creates

Henry Clerval
(Innocent childhood friend and traveling companion of Victor; a Romantic figure who seeks foreign lands)

Elizabeth Lavenza
(Adopted by the Frankenstein family; nurturing female character who marries Victor)

William Frankenstein
(Youngest brother of Victor; first to be murdered)

murders

murders

murders

accused of murdering

Monster
(Hideous creation shunned and feared by his creator and humankind; seeks female companionship)

places locket in her pocket

Justine Moritz
(Frankenstein family housekeeper; unjustly accused of murdering William)

seeks friendship with

De Lacey Family
(Blind father, son Felix and fiancée Safie, and daughter Agatha; respected Parisian family who risks their wealth to help Safie's father, only to be betrayed by him; the "monster" performs good deeds for them only to be spurned in return)

CRITICAL COMMENTARIES

The sections that follow provide great tools for supplementing your reading of *Frankenstein*. First, in order to enhance your understanding of and enjoyment from reading, we provide quick summaries in case you have difficulty when you read the original literary work. Each summary is followed by commentary: literary devices, character analyses, themes, and so on. Keep in mind that the interpretations here are solely those of the author of this study guide and are used to jumpstart your thinking about the work. No single interpretation of a complex work like *Frankenstein* is infallible or exhaustive, and you'll likely find that you interpret portions of the work differently from the author of this study guide. Read the original work and determine your own interpretations, referring to these Notes for supplemental meanings only.

Preface to the 1817 Edition

Percy Bysshe Shelley wrote the Preface to Mary Shelley's *Frankenstein* in September 1817. It immediately alludes to a "Dr. (Erasmus) Darwin," which gives some medical and scientific credence to the novel that it might not have had. Percy Shelley also mentions the German philosophical writers who, at the time, were experimenting with novels that touched on the Gothic genre, the science fiction genre, and the medical genre. Percy Shelley attempts to put *Frankenstein* in the context of other novels. He does not want the novel to be just a "mere tale of spectres." Wishing for us to suspend our disbelief that the dead can be brought back to life, he sees this as a novel that is more universal in nature and that gives insight into the human condition.

Shelley aims to seek the "truth of the elementary principles of human nature" and supply some innovative ideas regarding those simple human truths. The allusion is to the age of Romanticism and the Gothic novel. Romantic novels concern themselves with passion, not reason, and imagination and intuition, rather than the logical. Gothic novels frequently deal with the supernatural and remote, far away settings. *Frankenstein* will not be different and will adhere to the simple rules of Gothic novels. Shelley invokes the great works of Greek and English literature to act as guides and as a guideline for this work. He cites Homer's *The Iliad*, Shakespeare's *Tempest* and *Midsummer Night's Dream*, and Milton's *Paradise Lost* as works that are worthy of imitation and serve as exemplary models. He hopes that *Frankenstein* contributes to the body of English and world literature, perhaps equaling those previously mentioned works.

Shelley tells briefly how the novel came into being. During the wet and cool summer of 1816, in Geneva, Switzerland, several friends gathered to create and tell ghost stories. Percy Shelley mentions himself, Lord Byron, and Mary. He omits mention of Byron's mistress, Claire (Jane) Clairmont and of another guest, John William Polidori. Polidori later published his own Gothic novel, *The Vampyre; a Tale* (1819). This summer meeting produced two of the most important characters of English literature: the Frankenstein monster and the Vampire.

Introduction to the 1831 Edition

Five writers gathered in Switzerland during the summer of 1816: Mary Shelley, her husband Percy Bysshe Shelley, Lord Byron, Claire Clairmont, and John William Polidori, Byron's friend and physician. Mary's publishers have asked her to tell about how her novel came to be written. She was only 19 years old when she began the novel. By age 21, she was acknowledged as the author.

Being the daughter of two famous parents, she was not destined to be a writer; it was an avocation that she worked at. She recalls as a child writing stories to pass the time and to amuse friends. Her only audience was the select few she allowed to read her writing. But, through it all, she continued to write stories of imagination and of the fantastic. These stories were not meant to be personal but works of flight and fancy.

Percy Bysshe Shelley encouraged her work as a writer. She remarks that she was less than enthusiastic about writing. Instead, she worked at home, traveled, studied, and read. It was a trip to Switzerland, however, that changed everything.

Mary, Percy, and her stepsister Claire Clairmont rented a small cottage on the shores of Lake Leman (now called Lake Geneva), near Cologny, Switzerland during the summer of 1816. Byron was working on his major poetic work "Childe Harold;" Percy Shelley was working on his poem "Mont Blanc;" John William Polidori began his *The Vampyre; a Tale* (1819); and Mary began work on her future novel, *Frankenstein*. Only Mary and Polidori, the least known writers, produced a full version of their ghost tales.

Mary tells a little about each tale that was concocted and what happened to the end result. All the others abandoned their stories when the weather cleared, except Mary. Conversations between Lord Byron and Percy Shelley fueled her curiosity and desire to create a good story: "One which would speak to the mysterious fears of our nature, and awaken thrilling horror done to make the reader dread to look around, to curdle the blood, and quicken the beatings of the heart." And so she begins her novel.

Letter 1: To Mrs. Saville, England

Summary

This first letter, written on December 11, 17—, is from Robert Walton in St. Petersburg, Russia to his sister Mrs. Saville in England. Walton is on an expedition to look for a passage through the Arctic Ocean to the North Pacific Ocean via the seas of the North Pole. Knowing the harsh climate and the dangers involved with making such a passage, he feels confident that a crew and ship will be found to make the trip, even after six long years of his own preparations. Walton recounts how he will not sail until June of the next year on his expedition, when the polar ices have thawed somewhat. Soon, he will travel to Archangel (now Ankhangelsk), Russia to finalize his plans and hire a ship. He tells his sister that if he succeeds he will not return in months or years. If he fails, he will be home sooner or never.

It was Walton's father who had told his uncle that Robert should not become a career seaman. Robert does so anyway after failing as a poet and inheriting a substantial sum of money from a deceased cousin. He relays to his sister that he has felt a sense of sadness at his own ignorance, and he wants to improve himself and expand his knowledge.

Commentary

Literary
Device

This letter and the following three, which begin the novel, use a literary device called *framing*, which, like a picture frame, sets up the major premise of the novel. Shelley returns the reader to the letter format at the end of the novel. This technique eases the reader into the story and adds a subplot that gives the main story texture and richness. The framing technique also makes the story more compelling because Walton will eventually see the monster at the end of the novel. The story about the creature would be merely hearsay if not for Walton's personal encounter with Frankenstein and his creation. Shelley uses Walton to add validity to the novel. Also, note that the letters to Margaret Saville in England have the initials "M.S.," which could also be interpreted as Mary Shelley's own initials.

Theme

Many Romantic writers at this time had little formal education. To make up for this lack of education, they undertook adventures to broaden the mind and soul. Shelley and her contemporaries were no different. A popular destination was the European continent. These adventures would provide a source for growth and material for writing, as seen throughout Shelley's *Frankenstein*.

Walton, himself, is a fairly typical Romantic character because he is educating himself and traveling for his own educational pursuits. Feeling sadness at his own ignorance and desiring to improve himself, he laments in his letter that "my education was neglected, yet I was passionately fond of reading. These volumes [of Uncle Thomas' journeys] were my study day and night" as a young man. To add to his practical education, prior to this point, he worked as a second mate on a Greenland whaling ship, where he became a fine and able seaman.

Explorers had tried and failed to make the journey from Russia to the Pacific Ocean via the Arctic Ocean. Adolf Nordenskjold later completed this expedition through the Northwest Arctic Passage in 1878–79. This expedition will pass close to the North Pole, a far flung region not yet fully explored or understood during the 1800s. The remote place settings, the Arctic Circle and St. Petersburg, are another example of an element in the Romantic novel.

Letter 2: To Mrs. Saville, England

Summary

Now that he has reached Archangel in March, Robert Walton finds himself lonesome. He works steadily to ready a ship and crew but yearns for someone like himself to pass the time. Writing letters to his sister eases the loneliness somewhat, but he desires friendship. He tries to dismiss thoughts of failure and will perhaps return home via a different route, a changed man. The captain and lieutenant are possible choices for Robert's companions, but neither seems to fulfill that role for him.

Commentary

Here several Romantic ideas are thrust upon the reader at once: first is the allusion to Coleridge and seafaring; the second, to regions that are "marvellous" and "mysterious;" and third, a quest for personal and factual knowledge. Also, a Romantic notion is that Walton is so open to finding a friend (showing his feelings).

Weather slows the beginning of the trip, but Walton reassures his sister that he will use caution and prudence. He alludes to Samuel Taylor Coleridge's poem, *The Rime of the Ancient Mariner*. This one poem helped launch the Romantic period and gives us a story of a man banished for killing an albatross while at sea. The poem is an extended allegory symbolizing the death of imagination in man and an embarkment on a quest for spiritual and intellectual knowledge. Coleridge, a Romantic writer, was a friend of Mary's father.

The discussion about his educational background seems to be a continuation from his first letter. He regrets, "Now I am twenty-eight and am in reality more illiterate than many schoolboys of fifteen."

He mentions his desire for a companion, by saying, "I greatly need a friend who would have sense enough not to despise me as romantic, and affection enough for me to endeavour to regulate my mind."

Letter 3: To Mrs. Saville, England

Summary

Now well into his voyage, on July 7 Robert Walton writes to his sister. A ship, namely a merchantman, returning to Archangel and then England will deliver the letter. Walton's ship now passes through ice fields and warmer than expected weather. He tells of normal ship operations in the Arctic Sea but of no incidents that are of significance. He tells his sister goodbye and tells of how he will succeed.

Commentary

Again, Walton tells of Romantic sentiments: how the stars, or nature, will witness his success and how he can keep going over the "untamed and yet obedient" regions of the North Pole. Walton states that his heart is "determined," his will is what matters, and that success or victory will be his. Confidence in the heart, not the mind, and free will are hallmarks of Romantic thought.

Letter 4: To Mrs. Saville, England

Summary

This letter, written on three separate days (August 5, August 13, and August 19), begins quietly enough when Walton describes how his ship is stuck in an ice field far from land. On July 31, the crew sees a man "of gigantic stature" trailing a dog sled team going north and passing to within one-half a mile of their ice bound ship. The next morning on August 1, the crew finds another man floating free on an ice flow near their ship. The survivor is Victor Frankenstein. After a few days rest, Victor begins telling his story to Walton.

Commentary

This chapter mixes Gothic and Romantic elements. The eerie feeling of the Arctic, a Gothic notion, contrasts with the warmth Walton feels from meeting Victor and his desire for friendship, both Romantic elements.

Literary Device

The "being which had the shape of a man, but apparently of gigantic stature" seen by the crew is the monster. Since the crew has no way to follow the man due to the ice, they are bound to remain with their ship until the ice releases them. A few hours later, the late summer thaw frees the ship to sail free again. Here we have a sense of the eerie and sublime with a scene being played out in a fantastic place, the northern reaches of the world. The weather conditions suggest a sense of doom and mystery. The Gothic novel usually has a setting that is mysterious and foreboding.

In pursuit of his "demon," Victor is brought aboard the ship immediately and given comfort. Walton describes Victor as a "stranger [who] addressed me in English, although with a foreign accent." Two days pass before Victor begins to tell his story of how he came so far from land. He remarks to an officer that he "seek[s] one who fled from me."

Walton rejoices at the thought of having found a friend and confidant in Victor. Walton senses a deep passion and regret in his newfound friend. He says, "He must have been a noble creature in his better days, being even now in wreck so attractive and amiable." Victor remains on deck to look for the other sled as much as possible.

The August 13 letter shows how Walton esteems his new friend, Victor Frankenstein, by stating "my affection grows for my guest every day." It is now that Victor reveals his past circumstances: "'Unhappy man! Do you share my madness? Have you drunk also of the intoxicating draught? Hear me; let me reveal my tale, and you will dash the cup from your lips.'" Victor finds he cannot "begin life anew" because he has seen and experienced too much in his life. He hopes that by purging his guilt, through a confession, he will be able to meet the destiny that he knows he must meet.

Victor calls his best friend, Henry Clerval, a "wonderful man." He finds that Henry has a quality "that elevates him so immeasurably above any other person I ever knew." Henry also has "a quick but never-failing power of judgement" and "a voice whose varied intonations are soul-subduing music."

Victor sees the monster as his equal; he is even perhaps his superior, in every way. Perhaps this discussion is symbolic of the dichotomy of man. How can two equal halves of the human soul co-exist; that is, can good and evil co-exist in the same man? Can one half of a relationship be good and the other bad? Shelley's answer is found in the novel.

From a Freudian viewpoint, Victor is the *id*, the one who acts out his sexual and aggressive natures by seeking to become God. The monster represents the *ego*, which must work with the demands of the real world and how he comes to terms with societal rejection. Walton could be seen as the *superego*, or the conscience that regulates acceptable and unacceptable behavior. The three characters symbolize the struggle of man and his conscience with the good and the bad, the learned and the ignorant.

The August 19 letter has Victor beginning to tell his tale, and he emerges as the main narrator. He takes over fully telling the tale in Chapter 1. He cautions Walton against seeking knowledge too earnestly because of the results it may have. This caution is akin to the concept in Romanticism where the use of technology in the Industrial

Age can lead to disaster, if not properly checked by man. Victor advises Walton that "I ardently hope that the gratification of your wishes may not be a serpent to you, as mine has been."

Victor prepares Walton, and the reader, for what is to come by saying, "Prepare to hear of occurrences which are usually deemed marvelous." Victor further advises the reader to suspend his disbelief, because "things will appear possible in these wild and mysterious regions which would provoke the laughter of those unacquainted with the ever-varied powers of nature." He sees his only salvation being to "repose in peace." Resigned to this hard and fast fact, he foresees a coming confrontation with his creation, the monster.

Glossary

Here and in the following letters and chapters, difficult words and phrases, as well as allusions and historical references are explained.

pole the North Pole.

under-mate second mate, or second officer in command of a ship.

fortnight two weeks, or a two-week period of time.

capacious able to contain or hold much; roomy; spacious.

fosterage promoting, stimulating, or encouraging.

suppliant a person who supplicates; petitioner.

merchantman ship that carries commercial goods and passengers, not a warship.

paroxysm a sudden outburst as of laughter, rage, or sneezing; fit; spasm.

Chapter 1

Summary

Victor is now the main narrator of the story from this point on to Chapter 24. He begins his story just slightly before his birth. His father, although as of yet unnamed, is Alphonse Frankenstein, who was involved heavily in the affairs of his country and thus delayed marriage until late in life. Alphonse quits public life to become a father and husband.

Victor's father and Mr. Beaufort, his mother Caroline's father, had a congenial relationship. Mr. Beaufort and his daughter move from Geneva to Lucerne, Switzerland to seek refuge from poverty and a damaged reputation. Alphonse sets out to aid his lost friend to "begin the world again through his credit and assistance."

While in Lucerne, Beaufort had saved a small amount of money and had recovered his reputation somewhat, but he became ill and within a few months had died. When Alphonse finds the Beaufort home, he discovers an impoverished Caroline grieving at her father's coffin. Alphonse gives his friend a decent burial and sends Caroline to his family in Geneva to recover. During a two-year period, Alphonse visits Caroline and they eventually became husband and wife.

Seeking a better climate, the couple moves to Italy for a short period. During this time, Victor was born and lavished with attention. He was their only child for five years until Caroline comes across an impoverished family in need of help. She falls for a beautiful little girl who is Victor's age and asks the family if she could adopt her. The little girl, Elizabeth, becomes Victor's adopted cousin and playmate.

Commentary

Mary Shelley seems to pull her own experiences from childhood into the writing of Victor's background, which is the topic of this chapter. Mary Shelley came from a family of half siblings and a stepmother; Victor's family includes his two brothers and an adopted "cousin" Elizabeth. Mary's mother and Victor's mother also share an interest in visiting the poor. The care for the poor and the uneducated was a theme in Mary Wollestonecraft's life. Also, note that Elizabeth's mother and Mary's died during childbirth.

Theme

While on a summer visit to Lake Como, near Milan, Italy, Caroline comes upon a poor family who has five children to feed and little income. Mary's own mother was a champion of the poor and this autobiographical concept of her own life made its way into this novel. Caroline offers to take a girl child and adopt her for their own. The poor family reluctantly gives this adopted child, Elizabeth Lavenza, to the Frankenstein family. Elizabeth is almost the same age as Victor and described as "none could behold her without looking at her as a distinct species, as being heaven-sent, and bearing a celestial stamp in all her features."

Elizabeth is a beautiful and striking child. "Her mother was a German and had died on giving her birth," much like Mary Shelley's own mother, Mary Wollestonecraft, had done. Elizabeth is seen not as a mere orphan, but as a child the Frankenstein's had wanted for their own. Victor sees Elizabeth as a "pretty present" from his parents. Victor tells how Elizabeth was so much more than family to him; she was "more than sister, since till death she was to be mine only." These words have a true, ominous ring to them later in the novel.

Glossary

abode a place where one lives or stays; home; residence.

chamois a small goat antelope of the mountains of Europe and the Caucasus, having straight horns with the tips bent backward.

Chapter 2

Summary

Around the age of seven, Victor's younger brother is born. Up to this point, he and Elizabeth have been the primary receivers of their parents' love. Their parents decide to settle down in Geneva to concentrate on raising their family.

Victor introduces his life-long friend Henry Clerval, a creative child who studies literature and folklore.

At the age of 13, Victor discovers the works of Cornelius Agrippa, Paracelsus, and Albertus Magnus, all alchemists from an earlier age. His voracious appetite for knowledge thus begins, and eventually leads him to study science and alchemy. At age 15, Victor witnesses an electrical storm that peaks his interest in electricity and possible applications for its use.

Commentary

Character Insight

Victor tells how he and Elizabeth are brought up together as "there was not quite a year difference in our ages." He is serious and loud as a child, while Elizabeth has a more calm and subdued personality. The reader now sees a small glimpse of Victor's obsession with knowledge and learning. It is not unlike Mary Shelley's own lust for learning as a child and as the wife of Percy Shelley. Victor is the seeker of knowledge, "delighting in investigating their causes." He seeks answers to what occurs in nature and the physical world.

When Victor's parents return to Geneva to settle down, Victor is more solitary, doesn't like crowds, and finds himself alone at school. He befriends Henry Clerval, a Romantic character, who becomes his life-long pal. Henry is a writer and poet, a more creative person than the scientifically minded Victor. Henry is fascinated with the heroes of Roncesvalles, King Arthur and the Knights of the Round Table, and the knights of the Crusades.

The reader now begins to see Victor's personality type as sometimes "violent and my passions vehement." He dislikes learning languages, politics, and government and instead chooses to throw himself into the study of science, which he calls "the physical secrets of the world." While Elizabeth and Henry pursue the normal activities of children, Victor wants to learn all he can about the how's and why's of the world.

Literary Device

At the age of 13, Victor makes a discovery that forever changes his life. A storm confines him to remain inside one day where he discovers a volume of Cornelius Agrippa's works. His passion for learning leads him to Paracelsus and Albertus Magnus, two other scientists from earlier days, and invigorates Victor into a serious study of science and its possible applications. He reads science books for pleasure and knowledge, seeking to improve his mind and stimulate his curiosity. He laments that his father "was not scientific." Victor "was left to struggle with a child's blindness, added to a student's thirst for knowledge." He also exults, "The raising of ghosts or devils was a promise literally accorded by my favorite authors, the fulfillment of which I most eagerly sought." This gives us an idea of where he got the idea to create his own creature. He goes on to say that, "if my incantations were always unsuccessful, I attributed the failure rather to my own inexperience and mistake than to a want of skill or fidelity in my instructors." This seems to tell us that he wasn't having any luck with the teachings of his "instructors," so he knew that there must be another way, which opens up the possibility of using another science, electricity.

Literary Device

At age 15, Victor witnesses a summer thunderstorm that arouses his thoughts about electricity and possible applications for its use. The storm indirectly gives Victor the opportunity to learn more about technology and science. The storm Shelley describes is much like the one she and her fellow writers experience during the summer of 1816. Victor sees how the lightning has the power of destruction when a tree near their home is destroyed from a lightning strike. This confirms his belief that electricity and "galvanism" are worthy subjects for further study. A visitor in the Frankenstein home explains the phenomena to the young boy, and it facilitates a change in his thinking.

Although the details of the monster's creation are not described later in the book, Shelley hints that Victor uses his knowledge from the science books and of electricity to create his monster. Shelley makes Victor's interest in these topics very clear, so that the reader can deduce that he will use this knowledge in his creation.

Victor becomes a student of mathematics and pure science, seeking to learn the most he can, while abandoning his earlier study of well-known alchemists. His mind is not eased but spurred on by his lust for all knowledge and learning. He sees his fate as sealed after this choice in life saying: "Destiny was too potent, and her immutable laws had decreed my utter and terrible destruction."

Glossary

galvanism electricity produced by a chemical reaction.

campagne open country.

filial of, suitable to, or due from a son or daughter.

vehement having or characterized by intense feeling or strong passion; fervent, impassioned, etc.

predilection a preconceived liking; partiality or preference (for).

preceptors teachers.

Chapter 3

Summary

Victor is now 17 years old and ready to become a student at the University of Ingolstadt in Ingolstadt, Germany (near Munich), but an outbreak of scarlet fever at home delays his departure. His mother and "cousin" both fight the disease; Caroline Beaufort Frankenstein dies, and Elizabeth recovers. Before Caroline dies, she reveals her unrealized plans for the marriage of Victor and Elizabeth by saying, "my firmest hopes of the future happiness were placed on the prospect of your union."

Elizabeth becomes the family caretaker upon Caroline's death. Victor finds it hard to say goodbye to his family and dear friend, but he sets out for Ingolstadt to begin his studies in science.

Victor meets his mentors, Professor M. Krempe and Professor M. Waldman, at the university. He does not like Krempe, but he does find Waldman a much more conducive and congenial teacher.

Commentary

Victor does not like Krempe or the subject he teaches, modern studies of natural philosophy. Krempe calls Victor's prior studies of alchemists a waste of time by asking him if he has "really spent your time in studying such nonsense?" Krempe tells Victor that he must begin his studies again and gives him a list of books to read. He also advises Victor to attend the lectures of Professor Waldman in the forthcoming days.

Victor's visit with Professor Waldman goes much different. He describes the 50-year-old Waldman as "his person was short but remarkably erect and his voice the sweetest I had ever heard." Waldman explains to Victor that alchemy was a false science and teaches him that while the alchemist's pursuits were noble, real scientists do the scientific, valuable work.

Style & Language

Perhaps Shelley is trying to tell us a bit about both men's personalities if we translate both names from the German language. *Krempe* is the brim of a hat, rather ordinary and mundane; the name sounds like the word "crammed." *Wald* is a forest or wood, and *man*, means woodsman or forester. A "wood" jibes with the Romantic idea of returning to nature or natural things, a good place to revive the spirit and spend time; thus, a man with the name "Waldman" would be a more kind and reviving spirit.

Victor sees this "new" science as the enemy to his "own" preconceived science and vows to prove that the alchemists were right. He says he felt as though his new teachings were like a "palpable enemy" to be reckoned with, and he pledges to himself to prove his detractors wrong, by saying "more, far more, will I achieve; treading in the steps already marked, I will pioneer a new way, explore unknown powers, and unfold to the world the deepest mysteries of creation."

Theme

Victor spends a restless night and pays Professor Waldman a visit. Here he finds a kindred spirit in his teacher, who does not ridicule his study of Cornelius Agrippa or Paracelsus but instead sees some value in their work. The contributions of these men are not lost in the body of general scientific knowledge. He encourages Victor to study "every branch of natural philosophy," including mathematics, by stating, "if your application equals your ability, I have no doubt of your success." He also gives the young student a brief tour of his own laboratory, taking the time to explain his work and the devices he owns. At Victor's request, Waldman gives him a reading list, and the two part company. The theme of the Romantic notion that technology is not entirely good enters the novel at this point.

Victor calmly recounts that his time was well spent and a portent of his future fate, by saying "Thus ended a day memorable to me; it decided my future destiny."

Chapter 4

Summary

Victor throws himself into his schoolwork, reading all he can about the sciences, particularly chemistry. Gaining a reputation as a scientist and innovator among the professors and fellow students alike. Believing his tenure at Ingolstadt was nearing an end, Victor thinks of returning home to Geneva. However, he launches into a new venue of scientific experimentation—creating life from death and reanimating a dead body.

Visiting morgues and cemeteries for the necessary body parts, Victor fails several times before successfully bringing his creation to life. His work does take its toll on him, affecting his health and powers of judgment. This gruesome work carries on through the spring, summer, and fall of that year.

Victor lives for his work and throws himself into his pursuit so much that he shuts off all contact with the outside world. In the second summer Victor loses touch with his family. Letters from home go unanswered for long periods of time, and he delays sending a message home as to his health or well being.

Commentary

Theme

Shelley combines several themes in this one chapter: the Romantic notion of technology as a bad thing, the allusion to Goethe's Faust, and learning and the use of knowledge for good or evil purposes. Her Romantic background draws her to state that technology is evil; it is man who must control the technology, not the technology controlling man. Finally, the creation of the monster is not described at all. Perhaps Shelley had not worked out the details of the creation or the description would have been too much for nineteenth century readers. The mysterious creation is a Gothic element.

Victor is similar to Goethe's Faust character who went on a quest for knowledge, made a deal with the devil, and is rescued by God.

Unfortunately, Victor does not have the benefit of divine intervention. Instead, he succumbs to the end that all men must face. Shelley also introduces the theme of using knowledge for good and evil purposes.

Victor's attention to the contrast between the living and the dead becomes an obsession. To study, he must experiment, and to experiment, he must collect samples upon which to practice. He looks at what causes life or death and states, "I saw how the worm inherited the wonders of the eye and brain." And from this restless pursuit, he succeeds "in discovering the cause of generation and life" and he becomes "capable of bestowing animation upon lifeless matter." He is now a creator of life. He is like Goethe's *Faustus*, a man eager for knowledge and experience that is good for mankind in the end. Faust is saved by God, unlike Victor, who is not saved and who knows he will perish without redemption.

Victor thought he was doing a service by creating a new human. He says, "A new species would bless me as its creator and source; many happy and excellent natures would owe their being to me. I might in process of time (although I now found it impossible) renew life where death had apparently devoted the body to corruption." This goes back to the theme of learning and the use of knowledge for good or evil purposes. This quote also shows insight into Victor's state of mind, how he had built up his own ego thinking that he would be revered by the creature(s) he creates. It makes Victor like a human god.

Victor admonishes his listener by saying "Learn from me, if not by my precepts, at least by my example, how dangerous is the aquirement of knowledge and how much happier that man is who believes his native town to be the world, than he who aspires to become greater than his nature will allow." Shelley warns her readers about how knowledge can be too much and can cause catastrophic problems. It is this creation of another race of men that Shelley seeks to place in the mind of the reader. It is also now demonstrably clear that death can be conquered, and that man's replacement as God is now complete.

Victor is changing into a different person. His work is taking over his health, even though he knows, "a human being in perfection ought always to preserve a calm and peaceful mind and never to allow passion or a transitory desire to disturb his tranquillity. I do not think that the pursuit of knowledge is an exception to this rule." But his work is taking over his life, and he knows it. He says, "every night I was oppressed by a slow fever, and I became nervous to a most painful degree; the fall of a leaf startled me, and I shunned my fellow creatures as if I had been guilty of a crime." The last line in particular, "guilty of a crime," seems important. Victor knows his work on the monster is morally repugnant and that if any person knew of his work, the outside world would be repulsed by the nature of his experiments.

Glossary

chimera an impossible or foolish fancy.

palpable clear to the mind; obvious; evident; plain.

countenance the look on a person's face that shows one's nature or feelings; the face; facial features; visage; a look of approval on the face, approval; support; sanction; calm control; composure.

charnel-house a building or place where corpses or bones are deposited.

dogmatism dogmatic assertion of opinion, usually without reference to evidence.

pedantry ostentatious display of knowledge, or an instance of this; an arbitrary adherence to rules and forms.

physiognomy facial features and expression, esp. as supposedly indicative of character; the face; apparent characteristics; outward features or appearance.

arduous difficult to do; laborious; onerous; using much energy; strenuous.

Chapter 5

Summary

Victor succeeds in bringing his creation, an eight-foot man, to life in November of his second year. Excited and disgusted at "the monster" he had created, he runs from the apartment.

He wanders the streets of Ingolstadt until Henry Clerval finds him in poor condition. Henry had come to see about his friend and to enroll at the university. Henry and Victor return to Victor's apartment to find the monster gone. Victor finds the disappearance of his monster a source of joy and falls down in a fit of exhaustion from the release of anxiety over his creation. Henry spends the rest of the winter and spring nursing Victor back to health after the tumultuous fall. Henry advises Victor to write home, as a letter had recently arrived from his family in Geneva.

Commentary

Chapter 5 is significant because it marks the beginning of the novel that Shelley wrote during her now famous summer stay in the Lake Geneva region (refer to the "Life and Background of the Author" section).

The Gothic elements that can be found in this chapter are the grotesque (description of the monster's features), the eerie environment (Victor's lab at 1 a.m.), the undead quality, and some type of psychic communication (Victor's feeling of being followed). Also, this chapter builds fear in the reader, another big part of Gothic writing.

The monster now begins to take shape, and Victor describes his creation in full detail as "beautiful" yet repulsive with his "yellow skin," "lustrous black, and flowing" hair, and teeth of "pearly whiteness." Victor describes the monster's eyes, considered the windows upon the soul, as "watery eyes, that seemed almost the same colour as the dun-white sockets in which they were set, his shrivelled complexion and straight black lips."

Here Shelley contrasts God's creation of Adam to Victor's creation of the monster. Victor sees his creation as beautiful and yet repugnant, versus the creation story taken from the Bible in which God sees his creation of Adam as "good."

Character Insight

In a distressed mental state, Victor falls into bed, hoping to forget his creation. He dreams of wandering the streets of Ingolstadt and seeing Elizabeth through the haze of the night. During the dream, Elizabeth then turns into his mother, Caroline, whom he pictures being held in his own arms. While holding his mother, he then sees worms start to crawl out of the folds of her burial shroud to touch him. He awakes from the nightmare and goes directly to the laboratory to see his creation.

In the morning, Victor wanders the streets, alone with his conscience. Shelley layers into the novel a passage from Coleridge's *The Rime of the Ancient Mariner*, which makes a reference to a person who wanders the streets with a demon or fiend following him. The significance of this excerpt from *The Rime of the Ancient Mariner* cannot be underestimated. The significance of this poem in relation to this novel can be interpreted two ways. In the Gothic sense, Victor relates to the Mariner's isolation and fear. In the Romantic sense, both the Mariner and Victor want the knowledge; however, unlike the Mariner, Victor's new knowledge brings a curse along with it.

At this point Henry Clerval arrives in Ingolstadt. Their visit is the tonic that Victor needs to remind him of home and not his earlier labors.

Character Insight

Henry remarks on Victor's condition, noting the disheveled look, his "thin and pale" condition, and tiredness. The pair returns to Victor's apartment to find the monster gone. This note of happiness sends Victor into a fit of joy, knowing that his creation is no longer there. Victor falls in an uncontrollable attack of exhaustion and stress. He explains the cause as "I imagined that the monster seized me; I struggled furiously and fell down in a fit."

Henry becomes Victor's caretaker for the next few months. Occasionally, Victor, in his delirium, talks about the monster, causing Henry to think that the stress is causing him to be incoherent.

Chapter 6

Summary

Elizabeth's letter is the kind one would expect from a concerned family member. It is full of news from home that delights Victor and restores him to better health. Elizabeth tells of Justine Moritz, the Frankenstein's housekeeper and confidant. Even though Justine was treated poorly by her own family, she is a martyr for being a good, loyal friend to the Frankenstein family.

Victor introduces Henry to his professors, who praise Victor highly. Victor and Henry begin their studies together, studying ancient and foreign languages in order to engage their minds. Both men are happy to be hard-working college students.

Plans are made for Victor to return to Geneva in the fall, after his spring recovery, but weather and other delays make the trip impossible, and winter sets in. He revises his plans to depart in May.

Commentary

Elizabeth's letter relates how Victor's brothers, Ernest and William, are doing, and how their housekeeper, Justine Moritz, is faring with her family troubles. The tale of Justine is important because it relates how she endured poor treatment by her own family, being accused of causing the deaths of several family members, and how she came to be loved and respected by the entire Frankenstein family. The fact that Justine was not loved by her own family, but loved and respected by Victor's is much like the distance and alienation Mary Shelley felt from her own family. Mary was not fond of her stepmother, nor was she close to her step-siblings. In fact, Mary was sent to live with relatives in Scotland to keep her away from her estranged family. Perhaps her Scottish relatives were more welcoming of Mary than her own family.

Henry removes the chemical instruments in Victor's apartment because of the reaction that Victor has at the sight of those lab apparatuses. When feeling properly recovered, Victor introduces Henry to his professors, Waldman and Krempe, who have nothing but high praise for their now prized student. For Victor, the praise is a bit much, because he has a big secret to hide.

Clerval induces Victor to study the Oriental languages Persian, Arabic, and Sanskrit to help move his mind away from the sciences. The two study and work together on their language studies, even comparing those languages and their works with the ancient Greek and Roman works. Victor has become somewhat of a literary critic at this point.

Victor uses a great deal of emotion in his discussion over the differences in languages. He says, "when you read their writings, life appears to consist in a warm sun and a garden of roses, in the smiles and frowns of a fair enemy, and the fire that consumes your own heart. How different from the manly and heroic poetry of Greece and Rome!" He has studied Greek and Roman literature for most of his school life. However, the Oriental languages and literatures seem more sensitive to emotion than the Western "manly" literatures. Instead of broad, sweeping speeches by the main characters in Western works, he finds more subtle, appealing discussions by characters who seem to echo Romantic sentiments.

Chapter 7

Summary

Victor receives a letter from his father telling him to return home immediately. William, the youngest in the family, has been murdered by strangulation. The family were out on an evening stroll near their home when the young boy ran ahead of the group. He was later found "stretched on the grass livid and motionless; the print of the murder's finger was on his neck." Missing was a locket that Elizabeth had given William of their mother.

When Victor arrives at the city gates, they are closed, so he must remain outside the city in Secheron until the gates are reopened at dawn. It is at this time that he realizes that he had been gone six years from home and that two years have passed since the creation of his monster.

While near Secheron, on Mont Blanc, Victor catches a glimpse of the monster between flashes of lightning. Having a nagging feeling that the murder of his little brother could be the handiwork of his monster, Victor questions, "Could he be (I shuddered at the conception) the murderer of my brother?" The monster disappears when he realizes that he has been seen by his creator. Now fully believing that his creation murdered William, Victor knows that he cannot reveal the source of the crime without some serious inquiry about his creation. Thus, Victor is torn between revealing the monster and risking inquisition on his past or letting the criminal justice system free the accused.

Finally at home, Victor engages in a conversation with his family. He learns that Justine is accused of the murder with circumstantial evidence. He relays his assertion of Justine's innocence and states that she will be found not guilty. His words reassure Elizabeth in a time of great need.

Commentary

Victor receives a letter from his father telling him to return home immediately because William, Victor's youngest brother, has been murdered by strangulation. The significance of the letter is that it is a turning point in the book, in which the monster now has a real presence in the story; he is a threat to his creator. Up to this point, the monster has been in the back of Victor's mind. Here the monster is asserting himself into Victor's life.

Literary Device

The setting and atmosphere sets the stage for Victor to see the monster. The reader expects something to happen because of how Shelley describes the scene. Also, it is interesting that lightning has such a recurring role in the story. It is first how Victor learns about electricity and gains an interest in natural sciences. Then, it is assumed that he uses electricity to "jumpstart" his creation's life.

Not only does Victor *know* that the monster is responsible for the death of his brother (psychic communication), but the monster was able to find Victor's family (via psychic communication). Psychic communication is a Gothic novel quality.

It is at this point that Victor realizes that creation is responsible for the murder of his brother. He cannot reveal the source of the crime without some serious inquiry about his creation of the being. Thus, Victor is on the horns of a great dilemma. The family must put their faith in the criminal justice system to exonerate the accused.

When Victor repeats his assertion of Justine's innocence, her father remarks, "She is to be tried today, and I hope, I sincerely hope, that she will be acquitted." Justine is already a martyr, in the Frankenstein family's eyes, in that she is willing to suffer the guilt for a crime she did not commit. Perhaps Shelley is making a subtle point about the criminal justice system in England during her time. The rights that are enjoyed today are not the same rights enjoyed in the late 1700s. This passage plays a commentary about the rights of the accused and poor in English society, which is obviously a concern of Shelley's mother and probably a concern of her own.

Chapter 8

Summary

The trial for Justine Moritz begins at 11:00 the next morning. Victor suffers silent torture while the entire scene plays out in front of him. Yet, he can do nothing to stop it. Justine carries herself calmly at the trial, answering the charges and getting a sterling defense from Elizabeth. Although Justine proclaims her innocence, she is convicted of the crime. Her sentence is to die by hanging the following day.

Elizabeth and Victor go to see Justine in prison where both learn that Justine had given a false confession under stiff questioning. Justine goes to her death with no fear, leaving Victor to ponder the deaths of two innocent victims.

Commentary

Style &
Language

The chapter is a commentary on Shelley's view of the justice system. In fact, the name Justine is probably word play on "Justice."

Victor is now suffering "living torture" for the consequences of his actions since his university days. He has witnessed how two people close to him die as a result of his actions, the creation of the monster. The trial opens with Justine appearing beautiful and calm, assured of her innocence. The prosecutor presents the evidence of a market woman who placed Justine at the scene of the crime and the picture from the locket given to William.

Justine expresses true remorse for the death of William, proclaims her innocence, and tells of how she became part of the crime scene. Justine tells that she had been visiting in a nearby village, left that house to return home, heard of the search for William, found the gates of Geneva closed, and passed the night in a barn. However, she cannot explain how the locket was placed in her pocket.

In Justine's defense, Elizabeth tells the court of Justine's character and how she doted on young William and the Frankenstein family. Elizabeth's words move the court, and she makes a good witness for

Justine's defense. Meanwhile, Victor anguishes at the thought of the monster, the death of William, and the innocence of Justine, by saying "Could the demon who had (I did not for a minute doubt) murdered my brother also in his hellish sport have betrayed the innocent to death and ignominy?" Justine is found guilty through this "wretched mockery of justice," and her sentence is to be carried out the following day.

Visiting Justine in prison, Elizabeth and Victor learn that Justine has given a false confession. She did so thinking that she would not face excommunication from the church and atone for her supposed disgraceful conduct. What is amazing in the ensuing conversation is Justine's claim of innocence and her calm demeanor even in the face of death—in her words, "I do not fear to die, that pang is past." Victor hides in the corner of the prison cell, where he "could conceal the horrid anguish that possessed" him. Justine goes to her death later that day.

Glossary

lassitude state or feeling of being tired and listless; weariness; languor.

languor 1. a lack of vigor or vitality; weakness. 2. a lack of interest or spirit; feeling of listlessness; indifference. 3. the condition of being still, sluggish, or dull.

florins a British coin originally equal to two shillings: coinage discontinued in 1971.

pertinacity the quality or condition of being pertinacious; stubborn persistence; obstinacy.

vacillating wavering or tending to waver in motion, opinion, etc.

mien a way of carrying and conducting oneself; manner.

antipathy strong or deep-rooted dislike; aversion.

perambulations walks, strolls, etc.

league distance of about 3 miles or 4.8 kilometers.

ignominy loss of one's reputation; shame and dishonor; infamy.

Chapter 9

Summary

Victor finds no relief at the end of Justine's trial. Haunted by the thoughts of how he ruined so many lives, he cannot sleep or rest. He sinks into a deep depression from which he cannot escape. He tries boating on Lake Geneva and a trip into the Swiss Mountains. He escapes to the Chamounix valley region to rest and recover his senses.

Commentary

Victor suffers from a deep depression, almost like a relapse to his previous attack in Ingolstadt after he created the monster. His father sees his son's anguish and comments that it seems that Victor is suffering too much. Alphonse does not know what Victor has created and endured for six years, including recent events. Alphonse tells Victor that he owes himself to seek out happiness "for excessive sorrow prevents improvement or enjoyment, or even the discharge of daily usefulness, without which no man is fit for society."

Character Insight

Victor seeks refuge in boating on nearby Lake Geneva. As a means of easing his pain, he even considers suicide by plunging "into the silent lake." His conversation with Elizabeth shows that even she is changed by the murder of William and conviction of Justine, that she is no longer the same and she sees injustice as part of her world. Victor admits that he is the murderer, and the thought troubles him deeply. She finds Victor's despair a bit too much and wonders about his sanity. Victor hopes that these murders will be the last. Ironically, these killings are only the beginning of the misery that Victor must endure. Also, it is ironic that Victor thinks about ending his life, when just a few years earlier he was determined to create life and dispel death.

Theme

To ease his troubled mind, Victor undertakes a tour of the nearby Chamounix valley, France. He hopes that a rest and vacation will do him good. The visit is characteristic of Romantic thought in that nature can restore and refresh the soul. Victor mentions the Arve River, "ruined castles," and the "sublime Alps" as a backdrop to begin his current healing. Shelley delves into a description of Victor's depression and despair; depression and despair are both popular topics of Romantic writers. Also, the restorative and healing powers of nature come through when she describes scenes of beauty and majesty that transport the soul to another place and time. This section of the novel is a prose version of Percy Shelley's poem "Mont Blanc." Percy Shelley also mentions these same points of interest and speaks to the beauty of Mont Blanc, one of the highest peaks in the Alps.

Shelley describes Nature, who has winds that "whispered in soothing accents," like a caring mother who tells Victor to "weep no more." With his senses overwhelmed by all that he has been through, Victor throws himself to the ground and weeps bitterly. Upon arrival in the town of Chamounix, he rents a room, watches a storm play upon the summit of Mont Blanc, and falls down asleep, finally resting and beginning his recuperation.

Glossary

Mont Blanc mountain in E. France, on the Italian border: highest peak in the Alps.

Chamounix valley in E. France, north of Mont Blanc: a resort area of the French Alps.

epoch a period of time considered in terms of noteworthy and characteristic events, developments, persons, etc.

precipices a vertical, almost vertical, or overhanging rock faces; steep cliffs.

omnipotence the state or quality of having unlimited power or authority; an omnipotent force; God.

aiguilles a peak of rock shaped like a needle.

Chapter 10

Summary

Victor takes a tour of a nearby mountain and glacier on Mount Montanvert to refresh his tortured soul. While on the glacier, the monster confronts his maker. Victor seems ready to engage in a combat to the death, but the monster convinces Victor to listen to his story. The two go to the monster's squalid hut on the mountain, and the monster begins to tell his tale.

Commentary

Victor describes the area near Chamounix and the glaciers that were in the higher elevations. He comments on how nature will sooth his pain, "They elevated me from all littleness of feeling, and although they did not remove my grief, they subdued and tranquillised it." He found peace in nature and finds the scenery comforting. This is an extension of the same idea from Chapter 9, that nature has the ability to restore and heal.

Literary Device

A storm arises from the mountain below him. Again Shelley is setting the scene for the events to come. The storm comes in, and the reader anticipates something is going to happen. This could possibly signal a confrontation with the monster, because throughout the book, Shelley has used the weather as a signal.

Victor describes a desolate scene, filled with ice, snow, and rocks, that parallels the descriptions of the North Pole earlier in the novel. There is always the possibility of an avalanche, a thought that appeals to Victor. Perhaps the avalanche, through nature, will assist Victor in getting rid of the monster or his own troubles.

It is noon when he arrives on the top of the mountain, when he sees "the figure of a man, at some distance, advancing towards me with superhuman speed." Feeling rage and contempt for the creature, Victor says he could "close with him in mortal combat." Victor tells the monster to "begone" or "stay, that I may trample you to death."

The monster pleads with Victor to be allowed to tell his side of the story. The creature asks that he be made a happy and docile being once again. He pleads, "I am thy creature: I ought to be thy Adam, but I am rather the fallen angel, whom thou drivest from joy for no misdeed." In these lines, Shelley alludes to the Biblical creation story of Adam and to Milton's *Paradise Lost*. The monster likens himself to Adam, the first human created in the Bible. He also speaks of himself as a "fallen angel," much like Satan in *Paradise Lost*. In the Biblical story, Adam goes against God by eating an apple from the tree and even though He banishes Adam from Eden, He doesn't speak harshly of Adam. However, the monster seems sinned against, hated by Victor, feared by society, and banished, and thus murders to get back at his God.

Theme

The Romantic Movement espoused the idea that man is born good, but it is society and other pressures that create an evil man. Victor even says "I ought to render him happy before I complained of his wickedness." Thus, Victor and his views on the monster correlate to this Romantic viewpoint.

The monster speaks eloquently enough to convince Victor to calm down and hear his case. He asks that Victor hear his "long and strange" tale. Convinced that they should settle this feud between them amicably, Victor follows the creature to a small hut where they pass an entire afternoon together in conversation. The monster is not what one would expect. Not only is he eloquent and educated, he speaks of being loved and wanting love. And Victor, at this point, is the opposite in that he can only think of hatred for the monster. Thus, Shelley makes the monster a sympathetic creature, not a horrid one.

Glossary

Arveiron Val d'Aosta region of NW Italy on the Dora Baltea River.

pinnacle a pointed formation, as at the top of a mountain; peak.

Montanvert fictitious mountain, possibly near Mont Blanc, translated means "Green Mountain."

precipitous steep like a precipice; sheer; having precipices.

Chapter 11

Summary

During Chapters 11–16 the monster is the narrator and begins to tell his tale to Victor. The monster begins his story by recalling his earliest memories and how he came to be. After fleeing the city and villages where he is not welcomed, the monster learns to live in the forest. Food is sometimes stolen, and shelter is scarce. He does manage to find a "hovel" attached to a small cottage. He fashions a way to see into the cottage and begins to observe the life of the De Lacey family—brother Felix, sister Agatha, and their blind father—who lives in the small home.

Commentary

The monster's beginnings are vague, as are the memories of most adults when they recall their childhood. He learns about his bodily sensations and the strange world around him. How the monster leaves Ingolstadt is not described, but the reader can assume it may be due to the monster's limited sensory abilities during this early period. The monster becomes a vegetarian, living off of the land and the food that he steals from others.

Readers cannot help but be moved by his descriptions of the De Lacey's family life and the monster's reaction to them. Shelley takes pains to develop a full account of the creature's adventures. She describes a pastoral family, living by their own volition, in a plain and simple life. Brother Felix performs outside chores, such as gathering wood for fire, and sister Agatha tends the garden and home. Their father, now blind, is the children's source of joy and inspiration. Shelley makes us want to know this family in all their rustic charm—the kind of people Romantic writers often wrote about and praised.

This small family exhibits the devotion, love, and care that all families should strive to achieve. These simple folk are celebrated in poems like "Michael" by Wordsworth and "Elegy Written in a Country Churchyard" by Gray. The Romantics celebrated the common folk in their works. They saw the farmer and the laborer as the best in man.

These authors were celebrating not the high aristocrats, most of whom history books are written about, but rather, the man who makes his living simply, while engaged in simple life.

The monster observes the De Lacey family for a long time, careful not to make them aware of his presence. It is a quiet time for the monster and he grows fond of his newly "adopted" family. This is the first time he feels love and he, "felt sensations of a peculiar and overpowering nature; they were a mixture of pain and pleasure, such as I had never before experienced, either from hunger or cold, warmth or food; and I withdrew from the window, unable to bear these emotions." Shelley makes the reader want to see the monster as a maligned creature, worthy of understanding.

Glossary

hovel a small shed for sheltering animals or storing supplies.

offals refuse; garbage.

Pandemonium the capital of Hell in Milton's *Paradise Lost*.

tapers wax candles, especially long, slender ones.

Chapter 12

Summary

The monster notices the care and concern the family has for each other, and he senses that there is a mood of despair among the younger family members. The family suffers from poverty and a lack of food. Originally a well-to-do family from France, the De Lacey's have been exiled from France to Germany. The monster learns the French language from the family and practices those words by himself. Desiring to keep his cottagers happy, the monster becomes an aid to the family by secretly hauling wood to the cottage and performing repairs, all under the cover of darkness. He begins to follow a routine of daily activity and time passes from winter to spring.

Commentary

The monster sees that the De Lacey family has it all, but cannot understand why they seem so depressed. In his opinion, the De Lacey's lack nothing, as they have a "delightful house" and every "luxury": fire for warmth, "delicious viands" when they were hungry, "excellent" clothes, companionship and conversation, and "looks of affection and kindness." The monster discovers that the De Lacey's depression stems from poverty and hunger, so he makes a vow not to steal any more of their food and chooses to help the family by gathering wood and repairing the house and garden.

Seeing his reflection in a small pool of water, the monster discovers himself for the first time and now knows that he is hideous to behold. However awful he appears to the world, it cannot stop him from being a good and benevolent creature, even in the face of tremendous adversity. At the time, he does not even understand the compliments that are directed towards him when he is referred to as a "good spirit" and "wonderful" person by the De Lacey family for easing their burdens. He even dreams of one day presenting himself to "his family," hoping that they will look favorably upon his good deeds, not at his outward appearance.

Chapter 13

Summary

The monster relates how Felix reunites with his lost love, Safie, a woman of Turkish descent. Felix had rescued Safie's father from death in France and had placed her in the protection of a convent of nuns. She arrives in Germany just barely literate. Felix is overjoyed to see her again. Safie makes an earnest attempt to learn the De Lacey's language, which benefits the monster in learning a language as well. While listening to the conversations in the house, the monster gets a brief but memorable lesson in the history of Europe. Content in his hiding place, he calls the De Lacey family his "protectors."

Commentary

Shelley advances two concepts in this chapter that are central to the novel: one is the use of knowledge for good purposes, to know the world around you; and, the second is to question the essence of man's good and evil tendencies.

Theme

Shelley wonders how man can be forever changed by the simple act of acquiring information about his world. How can we as learned humans forever change the nature of man? Can learning be undone or is it permanent once learned: "Of what a strange nature is knowledge? It clings to the mind when it has once seized on it like a lichen on the rock." This again is the "use of knowledge for good purposes" concept.

Shelley seeks to find out how man is a paradox of contrasts: "Was man, indeed, at once so powerful, so virtuous and magnificent, yet so vicious and base? He appeared at one time a mere scion of the evil principle and at another as all that can be conceived of noble and godlike." She is questioning the existence of good and evil present in all men. This is a concept that crops up from the story of Adam in the Bible and one of the questions posed by Milton in *Paradise Lost*.

Also, Shelley causes the monster to question his own creation. He realizes that he is different and does not fit into society, a thought that terrifies him. He seeks to rationalize his being, meanwhile answering his doubts with answers: "Of my creator I was absolutely ignorant, but I knew that I possessed no money, no friends, no property. I was not even of the same nature as man." The monster must wonder, "where do I belong in the scheme of life, with men or among the animals?" Furthermore, who were his family and did he have a mother or father? These questions serve to fuel his inquisitive instincts. Only through Victor can some of his doubts be answered.

Chapter 14

Summary

The De Lacey family history is told through this chapter. The monster tells that the family was once well regarded in France with wealth and social position. Felix aides Safie's father in a plot to subvert the biased French justice system and free the Turkish merchant from death on the gallows. The discovery of the plot by the French authorities causes the ruin of the De Lacey family, as the government confiscates the De Lacey's wealth for their aid in the escape of Safie's father. Safie also must endure her own trials to find her benefactors in a foreign country.

Commentary

The De Lacey family was in the upper middle class of France, with Felix serving as a civil servant and Agatha who was "ranked with ladies of the highest distinction." Safie's father, a Turkish merchant who had been a businessman in Paris for many years, falls into disrepute for reasons Shelley does not make clear to the reader. It is supposed that all Safie's father did was to suffer from a xenophobic—fear or hatred of strangers or foreigners—attack by local authorities. However, all of his property is taken away, and he is thrown into prison to later stand trial. Shelley's point here is that the monster is telling this story about the injustice that the De Lacey family has to endure. This gives him the idea that he's not the only one who has suffered from an injustice.

Chapter 15

Summary

The monster begins his own education, reading the books and notes that he found in Victor's jacket in the nearby woods. In the jacket pocket are Milton's *Paradise Lost*, Plutarch's *Lives of Illustrious Greeks and Romans*, and Goethe's *Sorrows of Werter*. The list is a virtual required reading list of books that are all influenced by the Romantic movement in England.

Plutarch compares and contrasts the lives of Greek and Roman statesmen or soldiers for historical perspective. Goethe's work is a novel of letters written by a youth who is very sensitive and steadfast, who kills himself after being so uncompromising and idealistic. Milton's book is about the creation story and Adam, which causes the monster to question his own creation and place in the world. Finally, the monster discovers Victor Frankenstein's own notebooks, which explain how the monster came into existence. The monster is both intrigued and horrified at learning how he came into existence.

The monster also sees that his "adopted family" is doing better with the arrival of Safie.

Commentary

The monster notices that all has become better in the cottage with "his family" since Safie has brought some servants and money. Since the cottage dwellers have reduced their stress levels, the monster turns his thoughts inward to ask why he does not have an "Eve"? His readings in Milton have prompted him to want a mate for his own. He says, "no Eve soothed my sorrows nor shared my thoughts; I was alone."

This is a central concern for Shelley's novel. It is a basic tenant of life that humans pair with mates of the same species. But where was a mate for the monster? This is a troubling thought for Shelley, her readers, and her monster character. The monster's lament moves and compels readers. It gives the monster pathos. The reader feels pity and sorrow for this inhuman creature. The reader is privy to his thoughts, cares, and concerns. Seeing the monster as a pitiable character, he deserves the reader's empathy. Shelley strikes this balance between Victor and the monster that both are to be pitied.

The monster wishes to know "his family" better, so he plans to somehow make his presence known to them. He waits for Felix, Agatha, and Safie to leave the elder De Lacey alone before making his entrance. The conversations between the monster and the father go well until the walking party returns. Felix beats the monster, who offers no resistance, and the creature leaves the cottage to return to his hovel.

Glossary

Constantinople seaport in NW Turkey, now called Instanbul.

condemnation a condemning or being condemned; conviction.

Mont Cenis Alpine pass, in the state of Savoie, in SE France; see also Monte Cenisio, from the Italian.

Leghorn a seaport in Tuscany, western Italy on the Ligurian Sea.

Lyons city in east central France, at the juncture of the Rhine and Sacne rivers.

viands food of various kinds, especially choice dishes.

gesticulations gestures, especially those made with the hands and arms, as in adding nuances or force to one's speech, or as a substitute for speech.

vestige a trace, mark, or sign of something that once existed but has passed away or disappeared.

Jura state of Switzerland; or a mountain range along the border of Switzerland and France.

syndic any of various government officials in some European countries, esp. a civil magistrate or the like.

epithets adjectives, nouns, or phrases which are disparaging remark, used to characterize some person or thing.

Chapter 16

Summary

The monster and Victor are caught up to each other in time by the end of this chapter. This chapter is pivotal in that it blends the two sides into one story.

The monster sees his family leave their cottage, so he burns it down and goes to live off of the land. His travels carry him near Geneva, where he meets William Frankenstein, Victor's youngest brother. Realizing who the boy is, the monster murders the child and plants the locket in Justine's dress pocket. The monster's final request from Victor is to create him a mate.

Commentary

In Chapter 16, the monster is the victim of an injustice again. After his "adopted family" rejects him, he seeks to find Victor in Geneva. Along the way, the monster is shot through the shoulder after he saves a little girl from drowning in a stream. Recognized and shot as a villain, he is not seen as the savior he really is. He curses all men and, "inflamed by pain," he vows "eternal hatred and vengeance to all mankind." He passes a fall, winter, and spring in the woods, traveling at night to reach Geneva.

In a search for food and shelter, the monster encounters young William Frankenstein and kills him. He claims, "I too can create desolation, my enemy is not invulnerable; this death will carry despair to him, and a thousand other miseries shall torment and destroy him." The monster takes the locket from William, goes into a barn for rest, and finds Justine sleeping in the hay. He puts the locket of William's mother into Justine's pocket.

Chapter 17

Summary

The monster and Victor finish their conversation in a hut on the slopes of Montanvert. This important chapter is where the monster confronts his maker with an all or nothing proposition: "make me a mate or I will destroy you." He convinces Victor to once again re-create the process first used on the monster. Victor sees the monster's point of view and agrees to create a mate for the monster.

Commentary

The monster tells Victor: "You must create a female for me with whom I can live in the interchange of those sympathies necessary for my being." Victor refuses and then later relents to the monster's wishes. The monster threatens "I will work at your destruction, nor finish until I desolate your heart, so that you shall curse the hour of your birth." The monster also pleads his case saying, "My creator, make me happy and do not deny my request." The creature further promises to move far away from continental Europe to the wilds of South America.

It is interesting to note that Shelley doesn't mention the monster's sexual needs although he wants a mate for companionship. The first letter written by Walton to his sister mentions this desire for companionship as well.

Victor has second thoughts only to be moved by the monster's arguments. At this point, Victor and his creation should be thought of as equals. What the monster lacks is a formal education and the knowledge to create his own mate.

Character Insight

When Victor returns to Geneva to make preparations, his family is alarmed at his "haggard and wild appearance." Again, Victor is plunged into the abyss of despair and depression.

Chapter 18

Summary

Back in Geneva, Victor begins to study how he will create a second monster; he wants to know the latest developments in the scientific community. He recovers himself and tells his father that he wishes to go to London on a tour. He promises his father that upon his return he will marry Elizabeth. In September, he leaves Geneva, travels through France to Germany, Holland, and then London. His best friend Henry Clerval accompanies Victor on his journey. The two arrive in London during the late days of December.

Commentary

Victor invents the whole travel episode to disguise the true nature of his work. He is torn by his promise to the monster and the knowledge that if he fails there will be dire consequences for his family.

The question in Victor's mind is will the monster follow or stay behind. Confident the monster will follow, Victor leaves Geneva knowing what task awaits him and summoning the courage to repeat his terrible experiment yet a second time. He is so distraught that the scenery does not cheer him.

Literary Device

Victor joins the exuberant Clerval, and they journey up the Rhine River to the North Sea. Shelley presents a travelogue of her own tour up the Rhine. She mentions the places along the way that are important to her: the vineyards, the sheer cliffs, the islands in the river, and the ordinary people who carry on their lives in such a beautiful land. Shelley even quotes Wordsworth's "Tintern Abbey," a major Romantic poem and an influence on the writers of the period. The parallels between Shelley's Germany and Wordsworth's English Lake District are noteworthy for their descriptions of pastoral scenes and soul-refreshing spirit, which are the essence of Romantic writing and thought.

Chapter 19

Summary

Victor and Henry spend the winter in London, touring that city and making plans to visit the rest of England. The visit delights Henry, while Victor broods and only visits the philosophers who have the latest scientific information. The two go to Oxford, and a friend invites them to visit Scotland. Here, Victor suggests they part ways; he carries on with his plan, unknown to Henry, and fixes upon a poor, relatively uninhabited island in the Orkney Island chain. Here, Victor can finish his work in solitude and out of sight of anyone who may suspect his intentions. He gathers the latest information about the advances in his field but remains a depressed soul with the thought of what he must do again. To Victor, this whole odyssey is like torture, as he must gather the raw materials for a second creature. Henry is not aware of Victor's determined efforts and carries out his part of the tour with joy.

Commentary

Victor wonders if his family is safe, not knowing the whereabouts of the monster for some time. He parts company with Henry, who wonders about Victor's state of mind, but expresses "return, that I may feel myself somewhat at home, which I cannot do in your absence."

Character Insight

At times, Victor works feverishly; at other times, he would not work at all for days. His mind and heart are in a state of confusion, choosing between two choices: "Finish the monster or destroy this creation?" His body is "restless and nervous." He looks forward to finishing his work with mixed feelings. He says, "I looked towards its completion with a tremulous and eager hope, which I dared not trust myself to question but which was intermixed with obscure forebodings of evil that made my heart sicken in my bosom."

The setting is significant to the book. Victor says "I thought of Switzerland; it was far different from this desolate and appalling landscape." He picks a desolate island in the Orkneys off the coast of Scotland. The reader does not learn how he finds body parts on a practically uninhabited island.

Chapter 20

Summary

Victor sets about his work, creating a second female monster. After following Victor and Henry through mainland Europe and England, the monster comes near Victor's workshop in Scotland to see his mate. In a fit of anger and guilt, Victor destroys the half-finished creation in front of the monster and tells the monster he will not continue. The threat the monster makes is an ominous one: "I shall be with you on your wedding-night." The monster then disappears into the night.

Victor now contemplates who will be the creature's next victim. He receives a letter from Henry Clerval urging him to come back to London to begin planning a journey to India. Victor rushes to leave his island within two days, once he dismantles the laboratory and hides the remains. He sets out in a boat around 2:00 or 3:00 a.m. to dispose of the remaining body parts. Once the task is complete, he lays down in the boat to rest when the rising sun and wind awaken him.

A storm pushes the sailboat out to sea, and Victor finds himself in a dire situation. He fabricates a sail from his own clothes to steer him toward a town near shore. Surprised to find the local folk hostile towards him, he asks, "Surely it is not the custom of Englishmen to receive strangers so inhospitably." A man answers "it is the custom of the Irish to hate villains." Victor is immediately taken into custody, accused of murder, and sent to the local magistrate, Mr. Kirwin, to await sentencing. Victor goes along peacefully.

Commentary

Victor has begun the process of creating a new female creature, when he realizes that he had been in a similar position three years previously: "I was engaged in the same manner and had created a fiend whose unparalleled barbarity had desolated my heart and filled it with the bitterest remorse." This guilt forces him to reexamine his past and present situations. He is distraught at the idea that the new creation may be worse than his first creation. The new creature may not agree to the promises made between Victor and the monster, and he ponders that "she might become ten thousand times more malignant than her mate and delight, for its own sake, in murder and wretchedness." Could he continue his work in good conscience? Perhaps his evil work could endanger the entire human race. Shelley does not tell the reader how Victor got the pieces to create a new creature.

Victor, giving up the work, says "[I] made a solemn vow in my heart never to resume my labours." The monster returns to Victor's laboratory to find out why Victor ruined his mate. The two argue, and the monster issues a threat of "I shall be with you on your wedding-night." The monster will fulfill his warning later in the novel.

Chapter 21

Summary

A body has washed ashore; the method of death is familiar, the black marks of fingers on the neck. Since Victor appears around this same time, several people put him near the scene of a crime even though he had not been present. At least two witnesses saw a large creature deposit the body of Henry Clerval on the beach and leave.

Mr. Kirwin, the local magistrate, suggests that the whole entourage go to see the body. Victor becomes violently ill and passes two months near death: "The human frame could no longer support the agonies that I endured, and I was carried out of the room in strong convulsions." Victor is held in prison, and Kirwin sends a nurse and doctor to return him to good health.

At the trial, Kirwin offers a spirited defense of Victor and manages to secure Victor's release when the court learns of Victor's residence on the Orkney Islands. The time of the murder and Victor's presence in his lab in the Orkney's proves that he did not commit the crime.

Alphonse takes Victor home. The pair travel from Ireland to Le Harve, France and overland to Paris for a brief stay.

Commentary

Character Insight

Victor is a wreck of a human being, having worked to create a second creature and enduring the toils of a prisoner. The "shadow of a human being," Victor is not himself because a "fever night and day" threatens his "wasted frame." Alphonse fears that his son will not survive the trek back to Geneva.

The ironic twist to the tour that Victor and Henry started is that they both wanted an adventure for pleasure and relaxation, but it has turned to tragedy for both, "You travelled to seek happiness, but a fatality seems to pursue you. And poor Clerval—."

Chapter 22

Summary

Victor and Alphonse travel from Le Harve, France to Paris. They rest a few days in Paris before continuing on to Geneva. Elizabeth sends a letter to Victor asking if he has another love. When he arrives in Geneva, he assures her that he is ready to marry her. Ten days after his return home, Victor marries Elizabeth. Knowing that the threat made by the monster still hangs over him, Victor leaves on his honeymoon not sure whether the monster will carry out his evil plan.

Commentary

Spent physically and mentally from his ordeal in Ireland, Victor tries to tell his father that he alone is responsible for the deaths of Justine, William, and Henry. Alphonse dismisses these claims as ramblings of his exhausted son. Victor even tells his father "how little you know me. William, Justine, and Henry—they all died by my hands." An emphasis on "my hands" can be made because it was Victor's hands that created the monster, although the monster uses his own hands to strangle his victims.

Elizabeth's letter to Victor questions whether the two will ever be married as promised. She wonders if Victor has found another woman, and he is injured by the thought that Elizabeth is having doubts about his true intentions. What really troubles Victor is the pull between family loyalty and happiness versus the sentence announced by the monster. He agrees to set the date of the wedding to Elizabeth ten days after his arrival in Geneva. Victor promises Elizabeth that he needs to tell her his "tale of misery and terror" after they are married. This foreshadows the events that are to come later in the novel.

After the ceremony, the couple travels to Evian for their honeymoon. The contrast between the joy of the wedding and the threat of the creature weighs heavily on Victor. He arms himself with "pistols and a dagger constantly."

Chapter 23

Summary

While Victor is prowling the halls of the inn where the couple was living, the monster makes good on his threat to Victor, enters their bedroom, and strangles Elizabeth. Victor shoots at the monster when he flees, but the monster gets away without being wounded.

When Alphonse learns of Elizabeth's death, he is overcome with grief and dies. Victor goes to a local magistrate and tells the entire story to him. With the local authorities hamstrung as to what their action should be, Victor sets off in search of the monster to exact revenge.

Commentary

At 8 p.m. on the day of their arrival in Evian, Victor and Elizabeth go to the inn where they expect to spend their honeymoon night. A storm arises during the night as Victor wanders the halls to look for potential hiding places for his foe. During this search, the monster steals into the Frankenstein's room and strangles Elizabeth, like his other victims. As other guests rush into the room, Victor tells of the presence of the monster and a search ensues. The grief overwhelms Victor and he falls down "in a state of utter exhaustion." He vows to return to Geneva to protect his remaining family.

Literary Device

The setting is key because the storm signals that something evil is going to happen (another Gothic element). Victor feels "exhausted" and mad after a murder; each incident of murder throws him off several months, but the monster waits for him to get better before hurting him again. This is a quality of Gothic fiction, the psychic communication between characters.

Character Insight

In Geneva, Alphonse learns of his daughter-in-law's demise and he dies of a broken heart a few days later. Victor's mind turns from a victim to a seeker of revenge, to avenge the deaths of his friends and family at the hands of his creation. He says, "I have but one resource, and I devote myself, either in my life or death, to his destruction."

Even when Victor talks to the magistrate, he mentions that he feels the monster is still lurking around. This is a common thread that goes through the novel. The monster knows where Victor is at all times, and Victor can sense when the monster is very close. This is another mysterious, Gothic element.

Glossary

exordium the beginning part of a speech (the opening part of an oration, treatise, etc.).

ennui boredom, weariness, dissatisfaction with life (weariness and dissatisfaction resulting from inactivity or lack of interest; boredom).

maladie du pays homesickness.

Chapter 24

Summary

Victor leaves Geneva forever, goaded on by the monster's laughter. A chase ensues as Victor tries to capture and kill the creature who has tormented him for several years. Victor chases the monster from Geneva south to the Mediterranean Sea. Both board a ship bound for the Black Sea, journey through Russia, and make their way north to the Arctic Circle.

The weather gets worse as the duo travels north. There is little or no food and fierce winter storms. The monster steals a dog sled team and is seen by local villagers to be armed and dangerous. Victor closes to within one mile of the monster when the ice on which both travel begins to crack and separate the two from each other.

It is at this time when Robert Walton finds Victor, with his dying dog team dogs floating on an ice flow in the Arctic Ocean. Victor encourages Robert to continue the fight to destroy the monster if he does not.

Commentary

Visiting the cemetery where William, Elizabeth, and Alphonse are buried, Victor wishes his dead family goodbye and vows to seek revenge for their deaths. He curses the monster and wants retaliation for all the sorrow that has come to him. The monster is nearby laughing at Victor, which spurs the creator to give chase to the monster in order to destroy him. The monster knows that Victor would be at the cemetery because of their psychic communication, a Gothic element.

The chase leads from Switzerland to Italy, from the Mediterranean Sea to the Black Sea, from the steppes of Russia to the frozen tundra of the northern reaches of land near the North Pole. Both Victor and the monster live off of the land, pausing only to replenish themselves when necessary. The monster leaves notes behind to inspire Victor on and to keep his wave of hatred going against his foe, "My reign is not yet over—you live, and my power is complete. Follow me; I seek the everlasting ices of the north, where you will feel the misery of cold and frost, to which I am impassive." The monster feels they "have yet to wrestle for our lives, but many hard and miserable hours must you endure until that period shall arrive." Victor cannot follow the monster without help of the notes from the monster and the villagers' sightings.

Victor even promises to help Robert from the afterlife to assure that the monster will die a sure death: "Hear him not; call on the memories of William, Justine, Clerval, Elizabeth, my father and, of the wretched Victor, and thrust your sword into his heart. I will hover near and direct the steel aright."

Literary Device

The desolate environment of the Arctic is a Gothic element.

Final Letters

Summary

In the first letter, dated August 26, 17—, Walton is now the narrator for the remainder of the story. Walton tells how Victor proves his tale by producing the letters of Felix and Safie. Victor tells Walton to learn from his mistakes, that knowledge for evil ends leads to disaster. Walton comforts Victor in his last days and the two pass the time discussing other topics, such as literature, when Walton notices that it has taken a full week for Victor to narrate this story. Victor tells Robert that he must carry on the mission to destroy the monster.

In the letter dated September 2, 17—, Walton grieves at the fact that he has found a friend who seems on the verge of death and that his own mission to discover a northwest Arctic passage has failed. He writes to his sister to remember him fondly and to wish her family well.

In the letter dated September 5, 17—, Walton writes that Victor is now dying, and Walton has a near mutiny aboard his ship. The crew wants the ship to return to warmer waters before the ship is crushed by the weight of the ice. Walton chides the crew for their lack of adventure, and they agree to rescind their demand to turn the ship southward to escape a certain death.

In the letter dated September 7, Walton is in deep despair, now far short of his goal. He informs the crew that they will return to England if they are not destroyed.

In the last letter of the book, dated September 12, Victor wants to remain in this inhospitable climate even if Walton's ship returns home. However, Walton cannot lead the men to their deaths. Victor will not return to Europe or England without confronting his enemy. Walton knows that Victor will die soon from exhaustion and exposure. In the end, Victor dies.

The monster breaks into the ship's cabin where Victor's body lies in state. Walton and the monster startle each other and the monster begins to tell his part of the story when he began his reign of terror.

The monster finds that he can gain no sympathy from man, so he pledges to remain in the frozen north until he dies. The monster tells that he has suffered along with Victor and made evil his version of good. The monster promises no harm to Walton or his crew and leaves the ship to live out his days in the frozen land of ice. To the monster, dying is his only consolation to relieve the pain he has endured since he was given that spark of life in Ingolstadt. He swears "I shall ascend my funeral pile triumphantly and exult in the agony of the torturing flames." With this statement, the monster leaps overboard from the ship and disappears in the mist.

Commentary

The letters close the "frame" in the novel. Walton's version of the story is used to make Victor's story more believable. Walton gives some validity to the story by mentioning that he sees Victor's letters and the monster.

The first letter reinforces the theme that using knowledge for evil leads to disaster. Walton and Victor also talk of literature, probably Romantic books.

In the second letter, Walton has deep feelings about failure, sounding a depressed note on his failure to accomplish his goals. He also feels a deep sense of sorrow when he does find companionship, only to lose that companion in death.

In the letter dated September 5, Walton knows the limits of his personal and physical being, but Victor still wants to press on. Victor obviously has lost his mind, as no thinking person would risk their life for something like this unless it was really self-serving.

In the final letter, dated September 12, the monster alludes to Milton's *Paradise Lost* by saying, "But it is even so, the fallen angel becomes a malignant devil. Yet even that enemy of God and man had friends and associates in his desolation; I am alone." The monster knows that even the Devil had a host with him for aid and comfort. Being alone drove him to commit murders for revenge to torment his creator.

CHARACTER ANALYSES

The following critical analyses delve into the physical, emotional, and psychological traits of the literary work's major characters so that you might better understand what motivates these characters. The writer of this study guide provides this scholarship as an educational tool by which you may compare your own interpretations of the characters. Before reading the character analyses that follow, consider first writing your own short essays on the characters as an exercise by which you can test your understanding of the original literary work. Then, compare your essays to those that follow, noting discrepancies between the two. If your essays appear lacking, that might indicate that you need to re-read the original literary work or re-familiarize yourself with the major characters.

Victor Frankenstein **68**

The monster **68**

Elizabeth Lavenza **69**

Justine Moritz **69**

Victor Frankenstein

The creator of the monster, Victor spends most of the novel trying to defeat the monster. Victor is the oldest son of Alphonse and Caroline Beaufort Frankenstein. Victor's childhood is a good one. His doting parents lavish him with attention. He even receives a present, in the form of Elizabeth Lavenza, from his parents. Caroline Beaufort Frankenstein's last wish before dying is for Victor and Elizabeth to be happily married.

He later attends the University of Ingolstadt, where his interest in the teachings of the physical sciences prompt him to study them while there. He seeks to combine the best of old and new science to create a new being. Victor becomes obsessed with the idea of creating the human form and acts upon it. Immediately after creating the monster, Victor falls into a depression and fear. He leaves the university and returns home to his family, only to find tragedy there. Convinced his youngest brother's murderer is his creation, he sets off to find the creature.

Victor is a modern scientist unleashed upon an unsuspecting society. Not fully aware of the consequences of his creating a new race of humans, he spends his entire life trying to destroy the same creation. Victor is also the unbridled ego who must satisfy his urge to know all and use that learning to create a new race of man. His excesses ultimately destroy him. Victor represents the *id*, the part of the psyche that is governed by the instinctive impulses of sex or aggression.

The monster

The monster is created by Victor Frankenstein while at the University of Ingolstadt. "Formed into a hideous and gigantic creature," the monster faces rejection and fear from his creator and society. The monster is the worst kind of scientific experiment gone awry. He does acquire humane characteristics, even compassion for his "adopted" family, the De Lacey's, but he still murders for revenge. The creature also begins to learn about himself and gains general knowledge through the books he reads and the conversations he hears from the De Lacey's.

The monster represents the conscience created by Victor, the ego of Victor's personality—the psyche which experiences the external world, or reality, through the senses, that organizes the thought processes rationally, and that governs action. It mediates between the impulses of the id, the demands of the environment, and the standards of the superego.

Elizabeth Lavenza

Elizabeth Lavenza is the orphan child taken in by the Frankenstein family, who was lovingly raised with Victor; she later becomes Victor's wife and is killed by the monster on their honeymoon. Elizabeth was the daughter of a Milanese nobleman and a German mother. She was found living with a poor family near Lake Como. She was granted land, where she and Victor honeymooned, around the time she was getting married. Elizabeth is the one who keeps the family together after Caroline dies. Elizabeth survives the scarlet fever plague that takes Caroline. She writes to Victor while at school and tells him what is going on with the family. She is the source for information for Victor when he is away at the university. Her letters are important in the plot of the story.

Elizabeth also represents a character much like Mary Shelley herself, by aiding the poor, respecting all classes of common people, and coming to the assistance of Justine Moritz, when Justine is accused of murder. Elizabeth was a happy child and had a positive outlook on life. She is an innocent murdered merely for revenge on Victor.

Justine Moritz

Justine is the housekeeper for the Frankenstein family. We do not learn much about her character except that she embodies the best in suffering for a just cause. She represents graceful suffering in the face of injustice, much like a martyr. Justine is well treated by the Frankenstein family and is regarded not as household help, but with the esteem and affection accorded a family member. Also, Justine endures the rejection by her own family through no fault of her own. It is the Frankenstein family, specifically Elizabeth, who rescues her and allows her to continue her work as a housekeeper. Through the character of Justine, Shelley addresses the issues of equal treatment for domestic help and the accommodation of those in need of aid. Because of all that she endures, Justine is a sympathetic character who elicits a favorable response and empathy from the reader.

CRITICAL ESSAYS

On the pages that follow, the writer of this study guide provides critical scholarship on various aspects of Mary Shelley's *Frankenstein*. These interpretive essays are intended solely to enhance your understanding of the original literary work; they are supplemental materials and are not to replace your reading of *Frankenstein*. When you're finished reading *Frankenstein*, and prior to your reading this study guide's critical essays, consider making a bulleted list of what you think are the most important themes and symbols. Write a short paragraph under each bullet explaining *why* you think that theme or symbol is important; include at least one short quote from the original literary work that supports your contention. Then, test your list and reasons against those found in the following essays. Do you include themes and symbols that the study guide author doesn't? If so, this self test might indicate that you are well on your way to understanding original literary work. But if not, perhaps you will need to re-read *Frankenstein*.

Themes **71**

The Romantic Movement **72**

The Gothic Novel **73**

Plot **75**

Themes

Shelley makes full use of themes that were popular during the time she wrote *Frankenstein*. She is concerned with the use of knowledge for good or evil purposes, the invasion of technology into modern life, the treatment of the poor or uneducated, and the restorative powers of nature in the face of unnatural events. She addresses each concern in the novel, but some concerns are not fully addressed or answered. For instance, how much learning can man obtain without jeopardizing himself or others? This is a question that has no clear answer in the novel.

Victor Frankenstein learns all he can about the field of science, both before, during, and after his work at the university. Prior to his enrollment at the university, Victor focuses on the ancient art of alchemy, which had been discredited by the time of Shelley's writing. Alchemy was an early form of chemistry, with philosophic and magical associations, studied in the Middle Ages. Its chief aims were to change base metals into gold and to discover the elixir of perpetual youth. At the university, Victor gains new knowledge with the most modern science as a background. However, it is Victor's combination of old and new science that leads him down a path to self-destruction. This is one of Shelley's themes: "How can we harness the knowledge that we have so that it is not self destructive and for the benefit of all mankind?" The answer is not an easy one, and Shelley is not clear on her feelings about the use or abuse of technology. The reanimation of man from the dead is a useful thing to revive people who have died too soon, but what responsibility must we exercise once we bring people back from the dead? This is a morally perplexing question. Thus, we are stuck in a dilemma: "How far can we go in raising the dead without destroying the living?" Shelley seems to conclude that man cannot handle becoming both like God and a creator without much difficulty.

Since the Industrial Revolution had pervaded all part of European and British society by the time of her writing, Shelley questions how far the current wave of advances should push the individual in terms of personal and spiritual growth. She conveys the impression that perhaps the technological advances made to date rob the soul of growth when man becomes too dependant on technology. Personal freedom is lost when man is made a slave to machines, instead of machines being dominated by man. Thus, Victor becomes a lost soul when he tries his ghastly experiments on the dead and loses his moral compass when he becomes obsessed with animating the dead. Victor's overindulgence in science takes away his humanity, and he is left with the consequences of these actions without having reasoned out the reality that his experiments may not have the desired effects.

Shelley presents nature as very powerful. It has the power to put the humanity back into man when the unnatural world has stripped him of his moral fiber. Victor often seeks to refresh his mind and soul when he seeks solitude in the mountains of Switzerland, down the Rhine River in Germany, and on tour in England. Shelley devotes long passages to the effect that nature has on Victor's mind. He seems to be regenerated when he visits nature; his mind is better after a particularly harrowing episode. Nature also has the power to change man when Victor uses the power of lightning's electricity to give life to dead human flesh. The awesome power of nature is also apparent when storms roll into the areas where clear skies had previously prevailed. Victor ignores all of the warnings against natural law and must pay the ultimate price for the violation of those laws.

The Romantic Movement

The Romantic Movement originated in Germany with Johann Wolfgang von Goethe. Goethe's play *Faust* (1808–1832) addresses the issue of how man can acquire too much knowledge, how man can make deals with the Devil to get that knowledge, and how man can move from one human experience to another without achieving full satisfaction. Ideas about a new intellectual movement had circulated for some time in continental Europe and drifted across the English Channel to the islands of Great Britain. The earliest Romantic writer was William Blake, who was a printer by trade and whose works transcended art and literature. In England however, it was William Wordsworth and Samuel Taylor Coleridge's book of poetry, *Lyrical Ballads,* in 1798 that established the mark of European Romanticism on the British Isles. From this small volume, the criteria for Romantic writing were established.

Romantic writers are concerned with nature, human feelings, compassion for mankind, freedom of the individual and Romantic hero, and rebellion against society. Writers also experiment with the discontent that they feel against all that seems commercial, inhuman, and standardized. Romantics often concern themselves with the rural and rustic life versus the modern life; far away places and travel to those places; medieval folklore and legends; and the common people. Mary Shelley lived among the practitioners of these concepts and used many of these principles in her novel *Frankenstein*.

The monster is a Romantic hero because of the rejection he must bear from normal society. Wherever he goes, the monster is chased away because of his hideous appearance and his huge size. Shelley is attempting to show the readers how many people in conventional society reject the less than average or disfigured souls who live on the borders of our society. We cannot blame the monster for what happens to him, and Shelley elicits from the reader a sympathetic response for a creature so misunderstood. The monster tries to fit into a regular community, but because he is hideous to look at and does not know the social graces, he can never become part of mainstream society. The monster's response is to overcompensate for his lack of learning and then shun all human contact except when necessary.

Mary Shelley knew many of the famous writers of the time or knew the works of those authors intimately: Wordsworth, Coleridge, Byron, Keats, and her husband, Percy Shelley. Mary uses Coleridge's *The Rime of the Ancient Mariner* several times in her novel to align her misguided monster with Coleridge's ancient Mariner. Thus, she ties her novel to one of the most authentically Romantic works.

The influence of her husband cannot be disputed and is sometimes the subject of debate among literary scholars. How much did Percy Shelley influence the novel that his wife wrote? Some argue that Percy Shelley wrote the novel under Mary's name; others claim that he had a direct influence upon the writing of the book; while others maintain that Mary was the sole author, with some encouragement from Percy. Nevertheless, the novel was a work that was the product of an obviously fertile mind at a young age. From this viewpoint, *Frankenstein* is the pinnacle of Romantic thought and novel writing.

The Gothic Novel

Frankenstein is by no means the first Gothic novel. Instead, this novel is a compilation of Romantic and Gothic elements combined into a singular work with an unforgettable story. The Gothic novel is unique because by the time Shelley wrote *Frankenstein*, several novels had appeared using Gothic themes, but the genre had only been around since 1754.

The first Gothic horror novel was *The Castle of Otranto* by Horace Walpole, published in 1754. Perhaps the last type of novel in this mode was Emily Bronte's *Wuthering Heights*, published in 1847. In between 1754 and 1847, several other novels appeared using the Gothic horror story as a central story telling device, *The Mysteries of Udolpho* (1794) and *The Italian* (1794) by Ann Radcliffe, *The Monk* (1796) by Matthew G. Lewis, and *Melmouth the Wanderer* (1820) by Charles Maturin.

Gothic novels focus on the mysterious and supernatural. In *Frankenstein*, Shelley uses rather mysterious circumstances to have Victor create the monster: the cloudy circumstances under which Victor gathers body parts for his experiments and the use of little known modern technologies for unnatural purposes. Shelley employs the supernatural elements of raising the dead and macabre research into unexplored fields of science unknown by most readers. She also causes us to question our views on Victor's use of the dead for scientific experimentation. Upon hearing the story for the first time, Lord Byron is said to have run screaming from the room, so the desired effect was achieved by Mary Shelley.

Gothic novels also take place in gloomy places like old buildings (particularly castles or rooms with secret passageways), dungeons, or towers that serve as a backdrop for the mysterious circumstances. A familiar type of Gothic story is, of course, the ghost story. Also, far away places that seem mysterious to the readers function as part of the Gothic novel's setting. *Frankenstein* is set in continental Europe, specifically Switzerland and Germany, where many of Shelley's readers had not been. Further, the incorporation of the chase scenes through the Arctic regions takes us even further from England into regions unexplored by most readers. Likewise, *Dracula* is set in Transylvania, a region in Romania near the Hungarian border. Victor's laboratory is the perfect place to create a new type of human being. Laboratories and scientific experiments were not known to the average reader, thus this was an added element of mystery and gloom.

Just the thought of raising the dead is gruesome enough. Shelley takes full advantage of this literary device to enhance the strange feelings that *Frankenstein* generates in its readers. The thought of raising the dead would have made the average reader wince in disbelief and terror. Imagining Victor wandering the streets of Ingolstadt or the Orkney Islands after dark on a search for body parts adds to the sense of revulsion purposefully designed to evoke from the reader a feeling of dread for the characters involved in the story.

In the Gothic novel, the characters seem to bridge the mortal world and the supernatural world. Dracula lives as both a normal person and as the undead, moving easily between both worlds to accomplish his aims. Likewise, the Frankenstein monster seems to have some sort of communication between himself and his creator, because the monster appears wherever Victor goes. The monster also moves with amazing superhuman speed with Victor matching him in the chase towards the North Pole. Thus, Mary Shelley combines several ingredients to create a memorable novel in the Gothic tradition.

Plot

Frankenstein has three separate plot lines that circulate through the novel. The first is the Robert Walton plot line that introduces and closes the novel. Walton exhibits all of the emotions that we would expect from a person hearing such a fantastic tale. This plot line is like a picture frame, in which the accompanying story line is the virtual frame that surrounds the novel's main story.

The second plot line, and most important, is the Victor Frankenstein plot line. This plot line takes up much of the novel's volume.

Perhaps the most overlooked plot line, in terms of importance, is the monster's story. Mary Shelley gives the monster a voice, and the reader can sympathize with his pain and suffering at the hands of mankind. The portion of the tale dedicated to the story of the De Lacey family is part of the monster's story.

CliffsNotes Review

Essay Questions

1. Discuss what is meant by the Romantic patterns found in the novel?

2. Describe the personality of Victor Frankenstein and the monster he creates.

3. How does the monster learn about the world in which he lives?

4. Is the ending inevitable? Do the monster and Victor have to be destroyed in order for there to be order restored among men?

5. How is *Frankenstein* both a Romantic novel and a Gothic horror novel?

6. Discuss the role that nature plays in this novel.

7. Are the characters of Robert Walton and Victor Frankenstein similar or dissimilar? Discuss your viewpoint fully.

8. What is the significance of Milton's *Paradise Lost,* Plutarch's *Lives,* and *The Sorrows of Werter*?

Q&A

1. What is Victor's mother's name?

    a. Elizabeth Beaufort

    b. Caroline Beaufort

    c. Mary Wollstonecraft

    d. Elizabeth Frankenstein

2. Which university does Victor attend?

    a. University of Paris, France

    b. University of Geneva, Switzerland

    c. University of Ingolstadt, Germany

    d. University of Leghorn, Italy

3. Where does Victor go to perform his second attempt at creating a monster?

   a. Ingolstadt, Germany

   b. Ireland

   c. Geneva, Switzerland

   d. Orkney Islands, Scotland

4. What does Victor study at the University of Ingolstadt?

   a. English

   b. Natural philosophy

   c. Pure science

   d. Geometry

5. Who saved the De Lacey family from financial ruin?

   a. Victor

   b. Felix

   c. Alphonse

   d. Safie

6. Victor's two brothers are named _____.

7. Name the housekeeper for the Frankenstein family.

8. Name the two professors Victor knew at the university.

9. Name the magistrate in Ireland.

10. What was Robert Walton searching for in the Arctic Ocean?

Answers: (1) b. (2) c. (3) d. (4) b. or c. (5) d. (6) Ernest and William (7) Justine Moritz (8) M. Krempe and M. Waldman (9) M. Kirwin (10) A northwest passage to the Pacific Ocean

Identify the Quote: Find Each Quote in *Frankenstein*

1. "I am by birth a Genevese, and my family is one of the most distinguished of that republic."

2. "Of my creation and creator I was absolutely ignorant, but I knew that I possessed no money, no friends, no property."

3. "It is well. I go; but remember, I shall be with you on your wedding-night."

4. "I am practically industrious—painstaking, a workman to execute with perseverance and labour—but besides this there is a love for the marvellous, a belief in the marvellous, intertwined in all my projects, which hurries me out of the common pathways of men, even to the wild sea and unvisited regions I am about to explore."

5. "'My dear Victor,' cried he, 'what, for God's sake, is the matter?'"

6. "Fortunately, the books were written in the language, the elements of which I had acquired at the cottage; they consisted of *Paradise Lost*, a volume of Plutarch's *Lives*, and the *Sorrows of Werter*."

7. "I shall ascend my funeral pile triumphantly and exult in the agony of the torturing flames."

8. "My companion must be of the same species and have the same defects. This being you must create."

9. "Be happy, my friend: and if you obey me in this one respect, remain satisfied that nothing on earth will have the power to interrupt my tranquillity."

Answers: (1) Victor Frankenstein to Robert Walton, at the beginning of Chapter 1. (2) The monster to Victor Frankenstein describing his ordeal in Germany living outside the De Lacey house, Chapter 13. (3) The monster to Victor Frankenstein telling Victor of his plans for revenge, Chapter 20. (4) Robert Walton in a letter to his sister, Mrs. Saville in England, Letter 2, near the beginning of the novel. (5) Henry Clerval to Victor when he sees Victor for the first time in Ingolstadt, Chapter 5. (6) The monster to Victor Frankenstein, describing how he educated himself, Chapter 15. (7) The monster to Robert Walton, Chapter 24, letter dated September 12th. (8) The monster to Victor when the creature demands that a mate be created for him, Chapter 16. (9) Elizabeth in her letter to Victor, Chapter 22.

Practice Projects

1. Design a Web page based on the novel. Include links to all facets of the novel's composition, including Romantic fiction and Gothic fiction. Also include links to Mary Shelley on the Internet. Incorporate major and minor characters in the novel as well as elements of plot and setting. Describe the content that would be featured on the Web page.

2. Design a Web page that reinforces the key concepts in *Frankenstein*. Feature elements that challenge the reader to take a concept discussed to another level. Include a forum for discussion of key factors that make up the story. Dedicate a page to each major character and include minor characters. Include links to other Frankenstein sites.

CliffsNotes Resource Center

The learning doesn't need to stop here. CliffsNotes Resource Center shows you the best of the best—links to the best information in print and online about the author and/or related works. And don't think that this is all we've prepared for you; we've put all kinds of pertinent information at www.cliffsnotes.com. Look for all the terrific resources at your favorite bookstore or local library and on the Internet. When you're online, make your first stop www.cliffsnotes.com where you'll find more incredibly useful information about *Frankenstein*.

Books

This CliffsNotes book provides a meaningful interpretation of *Frankenstein* published by Wiley Publishing, Inc. If you are looking for information about the author and/or related works, check out these other publications:

The Annotated Frankenstein, by Leonard Wolf, ed., provides the original text of the novel and includes extensive annotations. New York: C. N. Potter: distributed by Crown Publishers, 1975.

Frankenstein, by James Reiger, ed., includes annotations and variant reading of the 1818 text. It also has the fragment written by Byron and the story Polidori wrote at the same time as Mary Shelley wrote her novel. Indianapolis: The Bobbs-Merrill Company, Inc., 1974.

English Romantic Writers, by David Perkins, ed., includes outstanding introductory material about the period, historical context, and literary scene. This textbook for college level classes is an anthology of major and minor Romantic writers. It does not include major women Romantic writers. New York: Harcourt, Brace, & World, Inc., 1967.

In Search of Frankenstein, by Radu Florescu, includes a filmography and an extensive bibliography. Boston: New York Graphic Society, 1975.

It's easy to find books published by Wiley Publishing, Inc. You'll find them in your favorite bookstores (on the Internet and at a store near you). We also have three Web sites that you can use to read about all the books we publish:

- www.cliffsnotes.com
- www.dummies.com
- www.wiley.com

Internet

Check out these Web resources for more information about Mary Shelley and *Frankenstein*:

Frankenstein, Penetrating the Secrets of Nature, `http://www.nlm.nih.gov/hmd/frankenstein/frankhome.html`—This Web site, created by the U.S. National Library of Medicine (NLM), combines the novel, impressive graphics, and a discussion of medical ethics in relation to the issues the novel raises about expanding the moral and ethical boundaries of medicine.

My Hideous Progeny: Mary Shelley's Frankenstein, `http://home-1.worldonline.nl/~hamberg/`—This excellent site, created by Mary Hamberg, details the biography of Mary Shelley. It also includes an electronic text of the novel, links to other *Frankenstein* Web pages, and scholarly examination of the novel and the persons connected to the novel.

The Gothic Literature Page, `http://members.aol.com/franzpoet/intro.html`. Excellent academic source for the Gothic novel genre. College level instructor Franz Potter has created an extensive list of Web pages, course syllabi, and texts that relate to the Gothic novel. Includes many authors who published Gothic novels from 1754 to 1818.

Mary Shelley and Frankenstein, `http://www.desertfairy.com/maryshel.shtml`—Superb collection of essays on the novel and ancillary topics. It has an excellent bibliography page for resources and academic essays that are useful in understanding the novel.

Resources for the Study of Mary Shelley's Frankenstein, `http://www.georgetown.edu/irvinemj/english016/franken/franken.html`—A good site by Martin Irvine that includes electronic texts of Mary's novel, William Wollestonecraft's work, Mary Godwin's work, and a review of film adaptations of the novel.

Next time you're on the Internet, don't forget to drop by `www.cliffsnotes.com`. We created an online Resource Center that you can use today, tomorrow, and beyond.

Films and Other Recordings

Frankenstein is an extremely popular subject for films. A string of films came out in the 1930s, and the interest of the story has prompted numerous others to pop onto the movie scene. The most well-known films include

Mary Shelley's Frankenstein, Tristar Pictures, 1994. A feature film directed by Kenneth Branagh features Robert DeNiro as the monster. The film follows the original text pretty closely.

Frankenstein, Universal Pictures, 1931. Another film that seeks to capture the essence of Shelley's novel. Considered one of the best adaptations of the Frankenstein novel.

The Bride of Frankenstein, Universal Pictures, 1935. In this film, Victor and his monster survive. When an evil scientist kidnaps his wife Elizabeth, Victor concedes to create another monster, a female companion.

Son of Frankenstein, Universal, 1939. Frankenstein's son Wolf arrives at his father's home. Wolf revives the creation, and the monster soon murders several villagers.

Other Media

Another good source for information is located at your local public or university library. It is a library subscriber service. Usually, the library or library consortium subscribes to the service with access given to patrons. Talk to your friendly librarian for help in accessing this resource:

Shelley, Mary Wollstonecraft. *Literature Resource Center*, the Gale Group, 2000. This database includes an author bio, a list of works, a criticism, Internet links, and other resources. It is excellent, especially when the library is closed.

Send Us Your Favorite Tips

In your quest for knowledge, have you ever experienced that sublime moment when you figure out a trick that saves time or trouble? Perhaps you realized you were taking ten steps to accomplish something that could have taken two. Or you found a little-known workaround that achieved great results. If you've discovered a useful tip that helped you retain information more effectively and you'd like to share it, the CliffsNotes staff would love to hear from you. Go to our Web site at www.cliffsnotes.com and click the Talk to Us button. If we select your tip, we may publish it as part of CliffsNotes Daily, our exciting, free e-mail newsletter. To find out more or to subscribe to a newsletter, go to www.cliffsnotes.com on the Web.

Index

A

abode, 24
Adam, 34, 44
adventures, 17, 18
Agatha. *See* De Lacey, Agatha
aggression, 21
Agrippa, Cornelius, 25, 26
aiguilles, 42
alchemy, 25, 28, 29, 71
Alphonse. *See* Frankenstein, Alphonse
American Revolution, 6
antipathy, 40
Arctic
    Gothic setting, 20, 64
    Victor chases monster to, 63
    Victor saved, 20–22
arduous, 32
Arveiron, 44
author
    biography, 2, 3
    career, 3, 4
    parents. *See* Wollstonecraft, Mary, and
        Godwin, William

B

Bible, 44
biography, 2, 3
Blake, William, 72
books, resource, 80
Bronte, Emily, 74
Byron, Lord, 3, 14, 15, 73

C

Caleb Williams, 2
campagne, 27
capacious, 22
Caroline. *See* Frankenstein, Caroline
    Beaufort
Castle of Otranto, The, 74
chamois, 24
Chamounix, 42

characters. *See also* individuals by name
    analyses, 68
    list, 10
charnel-house, 32
chimera, 32
Clairmont, Claire, 14, 15
Clerval, Henry
    described, 10, 21
    enrolls in university, 33, 34, 35
    irony, 59
    murder, 9, 59, 60
    removes instruments, 35
    Romantic ideal, 25, 36
    travels with Victor, 9, 55, 56
    writes to Victor, 57
Coleridge, Samuel Taylor
    as friend of family, 2
    Rime of the Ancient Mariner, The,
        18, 34, 73
condemnation, 52
Constantinople, 52
countenance, 32
creation
    monster, 8, 26, 31, 33, 74
    monster questions, 44, 49
criminal justice system, 37, 38, 41

D

Darwin, Dr. Erasmus, 14
De Lacey family, 9
    effect on monster, 45–47
    historical context, 7
    ruin, 50
    Safie's arrival, 48, 51, 52
De Lacey, Agatha, 45, 50
De Lacey, Felix
    beats monster, 52
    described, 11
    letters, 65
    reunites with Safie, 48
    romantic view, 45
    treason, 50
De Lacey, M., 11, 52
deaths
    Alphonse, 61, 63
    Caroline, 28, 68
    Elizabeth, 9, 61, 63
    Henry, 9, 59, 60
    Victor, 10, 65, 66
    William, 8, 37, 53

depressions
  Victor, 41
desolate island, 56
dogmatism, 32
Dracula, 74, 75
dream
  monster's, 47
  Victor's, 34

E

education
  man cannot become like God, 71
  monster acquires, 51
  nature of man, 48
  Romantic elements, 34, 71, 72
  Victor cautions Walton, 22, 66
eerie environment, 33, 74
ego, 21
elixir of perpetual youth, 71
Elizabeth. *See* Lavenza, Elizabeth
emotions, 19, 36, 46
ennui, 62
epithets, 52
exordium, 62

F

Falkner, 4
Faust, 30, 31, 72
fear
  Gothic writing, 33, 34
  Justine's lack of, 39, 40
  monster described, 33
  monster suffers, 9, 44, 68
  political revolutions, 6
  Victor's, 8, 9, 34, 68
  xenophobia against Safie's father, 50
Felix. *See* De Lacey, Felix
filial, 27
films, 81
florins, 40
foreshadowing, 26, 38, 43
fortnight, 22
Fortunes of Perkin Warbeck, The, 4
fosterage, 22
framing, 16
Frankenstein, Alphonse
  advice to Victor, 41
  background, 23
  described, 10
  dies, 61, 63

dismisses Victor's ramblings about
    monster, 60
  takes Victor home, 59, 60
  writes of William's murder, 8, 37
Frankenstein, Caroline Beaufort
  adopts Elizabeth, 23, 24
  described, 11
  dies, 28, 68
  marries Alphonse, 23
  Victor's dream, 34
Frankenstein, Ernest, 35
Frankenstein, Victor
  abandons unfinished monster, 57
  background, 8, 23, 24
  begins studying science, 8, 25, 26, 71
  character analysis, 68
  chases monster to Arctic, 63
  creates monster and runs, 8, 34, 74
  described, 10
  dies on Arctic ship, 10, 65, 66
  Elizabeth writes, 35, 36
  fear of monster, 34
  god, desire to create like, 31
  goes to college, 8, 28, 29
  Henry's murder, accused of, 59
  knowledge, obsession with, 25, 26,
      31, 71
  learns of Henry's murder, 9, 59
  learns of William's murder, 8, 9, 37, 38
  marries Elizabeth, 60
  meets monster, 9, 43, 44
  monster kills Elizabeth, 9, 61
  monster says he killed William, asks for
      mate, 53
  monster tells story, 45–51
  monster tells Walton about reign of
      terror, 65, 66
  monster threatens Victor, 9, 54
  nature, 72
  plans to create monster, 30, 31
  plans to create monster , 31
  plot line, 75
  relationship with Elizabeth, 25, 35
  relationship with Henry, 25, 34, 35,
      55, 56
  saved in Arctic, 20–22
  sinks into depressions, 41
  starts monster's mate, 9, 55, 56
  tells story to Walton, 20–22

Frankenstein, William
    death's effect on others, 39–41, 60,
        63–64
    described, 11
    murder, 8, 37, 53
French Revolution, 6
Freud, Sigmund, 21
friendship, 18, 20, 25, 72

G

galvanism, 27
gesticulations, 52
Godwin, William, 2, 11, 24, 81
Goethe, Johann Wolfgang von, 30, 31, 51, 72
gold. *See* alchemy
Gothic elements
    Arctic setting, 20, 64
    desolate island setting, 56
    eerie environment, 33, 74
    novels described, 73, 74, 75
    other Gothic writers, 14
    Percy Shelley describes novel, 14
Gray, Thomas, 45

H

Henry. *See* Clerval, Henry
history
    De Lacey family, 50
    Europe, monster learns, 48
    monster questions creation, 48
    period of novel, 6, 7
Homer, 14
hovel, 46

I

id, 21, 68
ignominy, 40
Iliad, The, 14
Industrial Revolution, 7, 21, 71
Instanbul, 52
introduction, 1831 edition, 15
irony
    travels, 59
isolation and fear, 34
Italian, The, 74

J

Jura, 52
Justine. *See* Moritz, Justine

K

Keats, John, 73
Keepsake, The, 4
King Arthur and the Knights of the Round
    Table, 25
Kirwin, Mr., 9, 57, 59
knowledge
    monster acquires, 51
    Romantic elements, 34, 72
knowledge, use for good and evil
    man cannot become like God, 71
    nature of man, 48
    Victor cautions Walton, 22, 66
Krempe, M., 8, 28, 29, 36

L

language
    German professors' names, 29
languor, 40
lassitude, 40
Last Man, The, 3, 4
Lavenza, Elizabeth
    character analysis, 69
    childhood, 23–25, 68
    defends Justine, 37, 39
    described, 10
    injustice, view of, 41
    letter about home, 35
    marriage plans, 9, 28, 60
    murder, 9, 61, 63
    Victor's dream, 34
league, 40
Leghorn, 52
letters
    Elizabeth writes to Victor, 10, 69
    monster learns of creation, 9
    monster learns of De Lacey family, 50
    Walton retells Victor's story, 8, 11, 17–21
    Walton writes of Victor's decline and
        death, 65, 66
Lewis, Matthew G., 74
Life and Adventures of Castruccio, Prince of
    Lucca, The, 4

lightning, 25, 26, 37, 72
literary devices
  foreshadowing, 26, 38, 43
  framing, 16
  setting, 61, 64
Lives of Illustrious Greeks and Romans, 51
Lodore, 4
lost souls, 71
Lyons, 52
Lyrical Ballads, 72

Magnus, Albertus, 25, 26
maladie du pays, 62
marriage plans, 9, 28, 60
mate, 9, 51, 52, 54, 57
Maturin, Charles, 74
Melmouth the Wanderer, 74
merchantman, 22
Midsummer Night's Dream, 14
mien, 40
Milton, John, 14, 44, 46, 48, 51, 66
Monk, The, 74
monster
  character analysis, 68
  creation, 8, 26, 31, 33, 74
  De Lacey family and, 45, 46– 48, 50, 53
  described, 10, 33
  education, 51, 52
  kills Elizabeth, 9, 61
  likens self to Adam, 44
  meets Victor, 43, 44
  psychic communication, 75
  Romantic hero, 73
  says he killed William, asks for mate, 9, 53
  seen in rainstorm, 37
  tells story, 45–52
  tells Walton about reign of terror, 10,
    65, 66
  threatens Victor, 9, 54
  Victor abandons, 8, 57
  Victor chases to Arctic, 9, 63
  Victor views as equal, 6, 21
Mont Blanc, 42
Mont Cenis, 52
Montanvert, 44
Moritz, Justin
  laboring class, author's view, 35

Moritz, Justine
  accused of William's murder, 8, 37, 38
  character analysis, 69
  convicted, 39, 40
  conviction affects others, 41, 60, 64
  described, 11
  joins Frankenstein household, 35
  monster frames, 53
  treatment of working class, 7
Mysteries of Udolpho, The, 74

nature. *See also* storms
  knowledge, 25
  power to change man, 72
  rejuvenating effects, 22, 41, 43, 71
  Romantic movement, 19, 29, 72
nature of man
  fears, 15
  Freudian ideas, 21
  knowledge changes, 48
  monster feels love, 46
  monster questions, 48
  Romantic ideals, 14
  Victor learns, 31
  Victor's creation vision, 31
Nordenskjold, Adolf, 17
Northwest Arctic Passage, 17

offals, 46
omnipotence, 42
Orkney Islands, 9, 56, 74

Pandemonium, 46
Paradise Lost, 14, 44, 46, 48, 51, 66
Paracelsus, 25, 26
paroxysm, 22
pedantry, 32
perambulations, 40
pertinacity, 40
physiognomy, 32
plot synopsis
  Elizabeth encourages Victor to come
    home, 35
  Justine hanged for William's murder,
    39, 40
  monster kills Elizabeth, 61

monster says he killed William, asks for mate, 53
monster tells story, 45–48, 50–52
monster tells Walton about reign of terror, 66
monster threatens Victor, 54
overview, 8, 9
Victor abandons unfinished monster, 57
Victor chases monster to Arctic, 63
Victor creates monster and runs, 34
Victor decides to reanimate a dead body, 30, 31
Victor delves into science, 25, 26
Victor describes childhood, 23, 24
Victor dies on Arctic ship, 65
Victor goes to college, 28, 29
Victor learns of Henry's murder, 59
Victor learns of William's murder, 37, 38
Victor marries Elizabeth, 60
Victor meets monster, 43, 44
Victor sinks into depressions, 41
Victor starts monster's mate, 55, 56
Walton writes about finding Victor, 20, 21
Walton writes from Arctic expedition, 16–19
Plutarch, 51
pole, 22
Polidori, John William, 14, 15
Political Justice, 2
poor and uneducated, treatment of, 24
Posthumous Poems, 3
preceptors, 27
precipices, 42
precipitous, 44
predilection, 27
preface, 14
psychic communication
    fear of being followed, 33
    monster finds Victor, 62, 63
    monster finds Victor's family, 38
    monster waits to strike until Victor recovers, 61
    Victor knows monster killed William, 38
psychology, 21

R

Radcliffe, Ann, 74
Rambles in Germany and Italy, 4
recordings, 81
Rime of the Ancient Mariner, The, 18, 34, 73

Romantic elements, 14
    adventures, 17, 18
    emotion versus intelligence, 19, 36
    friendship, 18, 20, 25, 72
    history of movement, 15, 72
    knowledge, 34, 72
    monster's reading list, 51
    nature, 29, 42, 72
    resources, 80
    rustic charm, 45, 46, 55, 72
    seafaring, 18
    setting, 56
    society creates evil men, 44
    technology, evils of, 21, 29, 30
Roncesvalles, 25
rustic charm, 45, 46, 55, 72

S

Safie, 48, 50–52
Satan, 44
Saville, Margaret, 11, 16, 17
seafaring, 18
setting
    Gothic novels, 14, 20, 56, 61, 74
    island in Orkneys, 56
    Romantic novels, 17, 56
    storm, 61
sexual needs, 21, 54
Shakespeare, William, 14
Shelley, Mary
    biographical parallels in novel, 35, 38
    biography, 2, 3
    career, 4
    parents. *See* Godwin, Mary, and Wollestonecraft, William
Shelley, Percy Bysshe
    marriage to Mary, 2, 3, 25
    novel's authorship, 73
    poem, prose version, 42
    preface to 1817 edition, 14
    Romantic movement, 7, 73
    workers, treatment of, 7
Shelley, Sir Timothy, 3
Sorrows of Werter, 51
storms
    Arctic, 63
    honeymoon night, 61
    nature's power, 72
    Victor meets monster, 43
    Victor recuperates, 42
    Victor sees monster, 37
    Victor swept to Ireland, 9, 57

superego, 21
suppliant, 22
Switzerland, 52
syndic, 52

T

taper, 46
technology, evils of
    lost souls, 71
    man needs to control, 30
    Victor cautions Walton, 21
    Victor delves into science, 29
Tempest, 14
themes
    adventures, 17
    dichotomy of man, 21
    knowledge, use for good and evil, 30, 31,
        48, 66, 71
    nature, 42, 72
    poor and uneducated, treatment of, 6, 24
    society creates evil men, 44
    technology, evils of, 21, 29, 30, 71
Transylvania, 74
Turkey, 52

U

undead quality, 33, 74, 75
under-mate, 22
uneducated, treatment of
    themes, 6, 24
University of Ingolstadt, 28, 68

V

vacillating, 40
Valperga, 3, 4
Vampyre; a Tale, The, 14, 15
vehement, 27
vestige, 52
viands, 52
Victor. *See* Frankenstein, Victor
Vindication of the Rights of Women, A, 2

W

Waldman, M., 8, 28, 36
Walpole, Horace, 74
Walton, Robert
    described, 11
    letter describing Arctic, 8, 16, 17
    meets Victor, 8, 20, 21, 63, 66
    monster tells story, 10, 66
    plot line, 75
    Romantic ideals, 18, 19
Westbrook, Harriet, 2
Westminster Review, 4
William. *See* Frankenstein, William
Wollstonecraft, Mary, 2, 6, 81
Wordsworth, William, 45, 55, 72
Wuthering Heights, 74

X

xenophobia, 50

CliffsNotes

LITERATURE NOTES

Absalom, Absalom!
The Aeneid
Agamemnon
Alice in Wonderland
All the King's Men
All the Pretty Horses
All Quiet on the
    Western Front
All's Well &
    Merry Wives
American Poets of the
    20th Century
American Tragedy
Animal Farm
Anna Karenina
Anthem
Antony and Cleopatra
Aristotle's Ethics
As I Lay Dying
The Assistant
As You Like It
Atlas Shrugged
Autobiography of
    Ben Franklin
Autobiography of
    Malcolm X
The Awakening
Babbit
Bartleby & Benito
    Cereno
The Bean Trees
The Bear
The Bell Jar
Beloved
Beowulf
The Bible
Billy Budd & Typee
Black Boy
Black Like Me
Bleak House
Bless Me, Ultima
The Bluest Eye & Sula
Brave New World
The Brothers Karamazov

The Call of the Wild &
    White Fang
Candide
The Canterbury Tales
Catch-22
Catcher in the Rye
The Chosen
The Color Purple
Comedy of Errors…
Connecticut Yankee
The Contender
The Count of
    Monte Cristo
Crime and Punishment
The Crucible
Cry, the Beloved
    Country
Cyrano de Bergerac
Daisy Miller &
    Turn…Screw
David Copperfield
Death of a Salesman
The Deerslayer
Diary of Anne Frank
Divine Comedy-I.
    Inferno
Divine Comedy-II.
    Purgatorio
Divine Comedy-III.
    Paradiso
Doctor Faustus
Dr. Jekyll and Mr. Hyde
Don Juan
Don Quixote
Dracula
Electra & Medea
Emerson's Essays
Emily Dickinson Poems
Emma
Ethan Frome
The Faerie Queene
Fahrenheit 451
Far from the Madding
    Crowd
A Farewell to Arms
Farewell to Manzanar
Fathers and Sons
Faulkner's Short Stories

Faust Pt. I & Pt. II
The Federalist
Flowers for Algernon
For Whom the Bell Tolls
The Fountainhead
Frankenstein
The French
    Lieutenant's Woman
The Giver
Glass Menagerie &
    Streetcar
Go Down, Moses
The Good Earth
The Grapes of Wrath
Great Expectations
The Great Gatsby
Greek Classics
Gulliver's Travels
Hamlet
The Handmaid's Tale
Hard Times
Heart of Darkness &
    Secret Sharer
Hemingway's
    Short Stories
Henry IV Part 1
Henry IV Part 2
Henry V
House Made of Dawn
The House of the
    Seven Gables
Huckleberry Finn
I Know Why the
    Caged Bird Sings
Ibsen's Plays I
Ibsen's Plays II
The Idiot
Idylls of the King
The Iliad
Incidents in the Life of
    a Slave Girl
Inherit the Wind
Invisible Man
Ivanhoe
Jane Eyre
Joseph Andrews
The Joy Luck Club
Jude the Obscure

Julius Caesar
The Jungle
Kafka's Short Stories
Keats & Shelley
The Killer Angels
King Lear
The Kitchen God's Wife
The Last of the
    Mohicans
Le Morte d'Arthur
Leaves of Grass
Les Miserables
A Lesson Before Dying
Light in August
The Light in the Forest
Lord Jim
Lord of the Flies
The Lord of the Rings
Lost Horizon
Lysistrata & Other
    Comedies
Macbeth
Madame Bovary
Main Street
The Mayor of
    Casterbridge
Measure for Measure
The Merchant
    of Venice
Middlemarch
A Midsummer Night's
    Dream
The Mill on the Floss
Moby-Dick
Moll Flanders
Mrs. Dalloway
Much Ado About
    Nothing
My Ántonia
Mythology
Narr. …Frederick
    Douglass
Native Son
New Testament
Night
1984
Notes from the
    Underground

The Odyssey
Oedipus Trilogy
Of Human Bondage
Of Mice and Men
The Old Man and
    the Sea
Old Testament
Oliver Twist
The Once and
    Future King
One Day in the Life of
    Ivan Denisovich
One Flew Over the
    Cuckoo's Nest
100 Years of Solitude
O'Neill's Plays
Othello
Our Town
The Outsiders
The Ox Bow Incident
Paradise Lost
A Passage to India
The Pearl
The Pickwick Papers
The Picture of
    Dorian Gray
Pilgrim's Progress
The Plague
Plato's Euthyphro…
Plato's The Republic
Poe's Short Stories
A Portrait of the
    Artist…
The Portrait of a Lady
The Power and
    the Glory
Pride and Prejudice
The Prince
The Prince and
    the Pauper
A Raisin in the Sun
The Red Badge of
    Courage
The Red Pony
The Return of the
    Native
Richard II
Richard III

The Rise of
    Silas Lapham
Robinson Crusoe
Roman Classics
Romeo and Juliet
The Scarlet Letter
A Separate Peace
Shakespeare's
    Comedies
Shakespeare's Histories
Shakespeare's
    Minor Plays
Shakespeare's Sonnets
Shakespeare's Tragedies
Shaw's Pygmalion &
    Arms…
Silas Marner
Sir Gawain…Green
    Knight
Sister Carrie
Slaughterhouse-five
Snow Falling on Cedars
Song of Solomon
Sons and Lovers
The Sound and the Fury
Steppenwolf &
    Siddhartha
The Stranger
The Sun Also Rises
T.S. Eliot's Poems &
    Plays
A Tale of Two Cities
The Taming of the
    Shrew
Tartuffe, Misanthrope…
The Tempest
Tender Is the Night
Tess of the D'Urbervilles
Their Eyes Were
    Watching God
Things Fall Apart
The Three Musketeers
To Kill a Mockingbird
Tom Jones
Tom Sawyer
Treasure Island &
    Kidnapped
The Trial

Tristram Shandy
Troilus and Cressida
Twelfth Night
Ulysses
Uncle Tom's Cabin
The Unvanquished
Utopia
Vanity Fair
Vonnegut's Works
Waiting for Godot
Walden
Walden Two
War and Peace
Who's Afraid of
    Virginia…
Winesburg, Ohio
The Winter's Tale
The Woman Warrior
Worldly Philosophers
Wuthering Heights
A Yellow Raft in
    Blue Water

Check Out the All-New CliffsNotes Guides

TECHNOLOGY TOPICS

Balancing Your Check-
    book with Quicken
Buying and Selling
    on eBay
Buying Your First PC
Creating a Winning
    PowerPoint 2000
    Presentation
Creating Web Pages
    with HTML
Creating Your First
    Web Page
Exploring the World
    with Yahoo!
Getting on the Internet
Going Online with AOL
Making Windows 98
    Work for You

Setting Up a
    Windows 98
    Home Network
Shopping Online Safely
Upgrading and
    Repairing Your PC
Using Your First iMac
Using Your First PC
Writing Your First
    Computer Program

PERSONAL FINANCE TOPICS

Budgeting & Saving
    Your Money
Getting a Loan
Getting Out of Debt
Investing for the
    First Time
Investing in
    401(k) Plans
Investing in IRAs
Investing in
    Mutual Funds
Investing in the
    Stock Market
Managing Your Money
Planning Your
    Retirement
Understanding
    Health Insurance
Understanding
    Life Insurance

CAREER TOPICS

Delivering a Winning
    Job Interview
Finding a Job
    on the Web
Getting a Job
Writing a Great Resume